THE FATAL AFFAIR IN MONTE DIABLO CANYON

The Fatal Affair in Monte Diablo Canyon

The Convict Lake Story—Robbery, Murder and Vengeance in the Old West

James S. Reed

© 2013 James S. Reed
All Rights Reserved.

No part of this publication may be reproduced, stored in a retrieval system, or transmitted, in any form or by any means, electronic, mechanical, photocopying, recording, or otherwise, without the written permission of the author.

First published by Dog Ear Publishing
4010 W. 86th Street, Ste H
Indianapolis, IN 46268
www.dogearpublishing.net

ISBN: 978-1-4575-2256-7

This book is printed on acid-free paper.

Printed in the United States of America

For Buck and Joe

Contents

Introduction		xi
Prologue		xv

Chapter 1: The Backdrop 1
  1   "Breakin' These Damn Rocks Is Killin' Him"   2
  2   "The Blow Would Be Heard the Fartherest
      by Any Mortal Man"   5
  3   "Be Wary of the Thieves and Assassins That
      Infest the Place"   9

Chapter 2: The Railroad Comes West 17
  1   Setting the Stage   18
  2   United by an Iron Roadway   22
  3   Hard Country   34
  4   Reno: Born of the Railroad   42

Chapter 3: The First Train Robbery in the West 47
  1   "The Whole Goddamn Payroll"   48
  2   "God Almighty, Can You Believe It's
      Sixty Thousand?"   56
  3   "It Almost Took the Public Breath Away"   70
  4   "The Trial Was a Memorable One in the
      Criminal Annals of Nevada"   76

Chapter 4: The Break 81
  1   The Prison   82
  2   The Plot   85
  3   The Escape   90
  4   The Aftermath   96

Chapter 5: A Murder Most Gruesome 109
  1   The Devil Charlie Jones   110
  2   Crossing the Pine Nut Mountains   113
  3   Aurora and the Demise of the Daly Gang   122
  4   The Mail Rider Billy Poor   133
  5   The Funeral   143

Chapter 6: The Fatal Affair in Monte Diablo Canyon 145
   1   The Devil Mountain   146
   2   Morrison Spots the Convicts   161
   3   The Morning Hours   163
   4   El Diablo Has His Due   166
   5   Escape to Silver Peak   171

Chapter 7: Atonement 175
   1   "A Large and Grief-Stricken Circle of Friends
       Attended the Solemn Ceremony"   176
   2   No Country for Mean Men   178
   3   The "Trial"   187
   4   "And Such a Death"   189

Epilogue 197
   1   Renaming the Landscape   198
   2   Two Vile Men   200
   3   Vigilantism   203

Bibliography / Recommended Reading   207
Credits   210
The Author   212

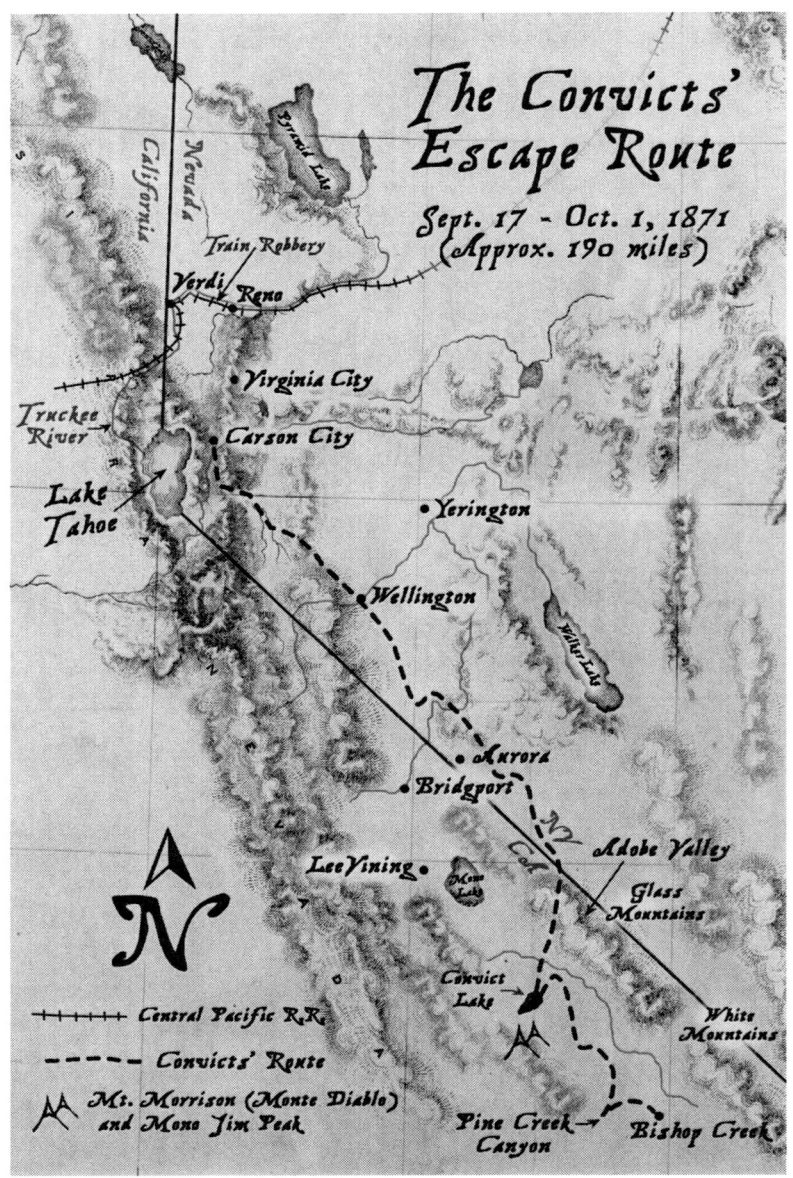

*Convict Lake with Mount Morrison (12241') at the right rear and Mono Jim Peak (10858') in the foreground.
(Courtesy of Rollie Rodriguez.)*

Introduction

In 1972 meteorologist Edward Lorenz of the Massachusetts Institute of Technology broached the term "butterfly effect" to highlight the possibility that small causes may have momentous effects. He was speaking of weather phenomena, and the question posed was whether the flap of a butterfly's wings in Brazil could result in a tornado in Texas. Lorenz's insights are anchored in chaos theory and have generated widespread scientific interest.

The butterfly does not cause the storm; rather, the flap of the wings is part of the initial conditions. One set of conditions leads to the tornado; the others don't. In other words, small differences in a dynamic system can trigger vast and often unexpected results. Depending on what one calls a "dynamic system," the butterfly effect is illustrative of the story told in this book.

A question implicit in the story is whether the births of three brothers in a small community in Indiana during the period 1838–43 were the initial conditions that ultimately resulted in the death of a merchant in Mono County, California, in 1871. The brothers, none of whom traveled farther west than Missouri, pulled off the first train robbery in the country's history in Indiana in 1866. In a copycat crime, a gang from Virginia City robbed the new transcontinental railroad in Nevada in 1870.

It's an interesting coincidence that the surname of the Indiana brothers was Reno, while the surname of their principal accomplice was Sparks. Thus, history's first train robbery was pulled off by Reno and Sparks, the names of neighboring Nevada cities near where the robbery described in these pages took place some four years later.

Convict Lake sits in a rugged canyon of like name in the Eastern Sierra near Mammoth Lakes, California. A plaque placed near the lake's outlet by the Mono County Board of Supervisors and E Clampus Vitus, a fraternal organization specializing in the history of mining regions of California and Nevada, tells the story of a deadly gun battle that took place near the lake in September 1871. Escapees from the Nevada State Prison who had holed up in the canyon got the drop on a posse out to take them dead or alive.

The lake is in what was then called Monte Diablo Canyon, hence the title of this book. The phrase "The Fatal Affair in Monte Diablo Canyon" is taken from an article about the battle that appeared in the September 30, 1871, edition of the *Inyo Independent*, the newspaper of record in nearby Inyo County. The likely author of the article was the editor of the newspaper, a historic Inyo County public figure who played a significant role in the culminating events described here.

Curious about the story told by the plaque, I began researching it in the Nevada State Library and Archives in the late 1990s. Articles in the September 19, 1871, editions of Carson City's *Daily State Register* and Virginia City's *Daily Territorial Enterprise* (Mark Twain's one-time employer) got me started. They describe a bloody gunfight at the state prison in Carson City and the ensuing escape of twenty-nine prisoners.

An article in Reno's *Nevada State Journal* on October 14, 1871, headlined "How It Was Planned and Executed," stated that as the prisoners discussed who should take the lead in planning and carrying out the prison break, "Jack Davis, one of the Verdi car robbers was named; but the 'railroad gang' ... objected to Davis because he had turned State's evidence on trial."

Now it became interesting. What was meant by "the Verdi car robbers"? Who were the "railroad gang"? What trial?

Sam Davis, in his *History of Nevada* and in a chapter titled "The Lawless Element," said that on November 1, 1870, Jack Davis "planned and executed the first train robbery on record" near Verdi. Thus, he said, "Nevada acquired the dubious credit of being the first in the Union that could produce a set of outlaws daring enough to stop and rob an express train."

Sam Davis's date for the train robbery was off by four days; moreover, Indiana had preempted Nevada by earning the dubious credit of producing the first outlaws who would dare to rob an express train. Nonetheless, the robbery of the Central Pacific Railroad's *Overland Express* by Jack Davis and his cohorts was the West's first train robbery. The robbers were pursued by a lawman whose dogged perseverance brings to mind Inspector Javert, Jean Valjean's pursuer in Victor Hugo's *Les Misérables*.

This was the thread of a good tale: a prison break led by men who had engineered the first train robbery in the West; some of the heavily armed escapees engaging in a deadly gun battle nearly two hundred miles to the south a week after the break. My purpose was to determine how and why this all started, how it transpired, and its ending, which, to say the least, was bizarre.

The story is told in the context of its time: the construction of the transcontinental railroad over the Sierras; gold and silver discoveries that hastened the building of the West; the boom-and-bust, often lawless, mining camps of Nevada; and the preference for vigilantism over tiresome judicial procedures. In some chapters a modified historical fiction approach is used to give some immediacy to the lives—and the anxieties—of the desperate men involved, two of whom were murderous psychopaths. The dialogue is based in part on first-person accounts published in newspapers of the day. I thought it appropriate that the participants have a part in telling the story.

Jim Reed
Mammoth Lakes, California

Prologue

"They Might as Well Have Pulled the Trigger"

Send me sixty dollars tonight without fail.
— J. Enrique

The coded message was telegraphed from San Francisco to Reno on November 4, 1870. The sender was signaling the man on the other end that a fortune in gold coin—he figured about sixty thousand dollars—would be on the next Central Pacific express train headed east over the Sierra Nevada. It was the crucial step in the conspiracy that resulted in the first train robbery in the history of the West and, indeed, of the new transcontinental railroad.

The message also sealed the fate of Robert Morrison, a popular young merchant and Wells Fargo agent who operated a general store in Benton Hot Springs in Mono County, California, some two hundred miles south of Reno. Nearly a year later, Morrison would be killed in a gun battle with men who had escaped from the Nevada State Prison in Carson City.

Neither the sender nor the recipient of the message knew or would ever meet Morrison. Both were in jail when he was slain.

The connection between the message and the murder was never made.

Yet the actions of the two conspirators were so much the cause of Morrison's death that they might as well have pulled the trigger.

CHAPTER 1

The Backdrop

1
"Breakin' These Damn Rocks Is Killin' Him"

John Chapman says, "Count me out if Davis is in on this one. He turned state's evidence once, and he isn't going to get another chance. Wasn't for him, we wouldn't be on this rock pile."

Chapman and his old pal John Squiers, the stage robber, had come up with the plan to rob the Central Pacific's payroll train. The other men had greedily, and naively, bought into it. Good detective work had nailed the robbers, and Jack Davis wasn't the only one of them who had copped out to prosecutors in exchange for a light sentence. Seven months earlier, on Christmas Day 1870, five of the robbers had been sentenced to long stretches in the Nevada State Prison in Carson City for pulling off such an audacious crime that, according to an account wired across the country, it "took the public breath away."

Now the talk is about breaking out. Chapman and Squiers are having a quiet parley with E. B. Parsons, another of the train robbers. They're off by themselves in the rock quarry at the foot of Prison Hill. They first have to decide who they can trust to bring in. Later they'll work out the details. Chapman sits on a rock; the others squat on their hams. They chew and spit as they talk.

"I want no part of Davis, but we should bring in Pat Hurley. He's a tough Irishman," Parsons says. "He told me he don't mind prison much as long as he gets his three squares, but he says breakin' these damn rocks all day is killin' him."

"Put him on the list," Chapman says. "I trust him."

Squiers wipes tobacco juice off his beard with the soiled, ragged sleeve of his ill-fitting prison uniform. "We should bring in Moses Black. He's dumb as all get out, but he won't talk and he's strong as a mule. Sure'n hell ain't afraid of no guards."

"We need the muscle."

A guard bangs a shovel on a rock. "Break's over!"

They're back slinging sixteen-pound sledgehammers. Squiers, perspiring heavily, yells at Deadman, the trustee making the rounds with the water bucket. "If you don't get over quick with that bucket, you won't be long for the world, and by God, I mean it."

"Go to hell, Squiers. Come and get it yourself."

Squiers knows Deadman can get him a stay in solitary. He glares menacingly at the trustee as he strides over to drink.

They're hammering out the rocks used to build the prison that houses them. They don't need the Irishman Hurley to remind them that quarry work is backbreaking. They were at it in January when blizzards were sweeping off the mountains, and they're at it now in the midsummer heat and swirling, blinding dust.

Prison life hasn't tamed many of the hundred men inside, yet their defiance isn't a result of the mean prison conditions. Most had worked at hard-rock mining or cowboying on the ranches in the vastness of the Nevada outback, where life was tough and free time meant drinking and brawling—and often violent death.

What eats at them is the debilitating boredom, the every day sameness. The endless passage of time evokes thoughts of the whiskey and women that freedom will bring. The risks of an escape attempt pale in comparison.

The Carson River is a mile east past Prison Hill. The men working the quarry welcome the breezes that blow up the river canyon. A quick bolt and run along the river road and across Mexican Dam will set a man headed south in the Pine Nut Mountains and then east into the unpopulated valleys and mountains of basin and range country, where the law will have a hard time tracking him.

Or a couple miles west and he'll be in the wilderness of the Carson Range and soon its more westerly and loftier sister range, the Sierra Nevada. Few who have been in the prison have gazed at the towering mountains without thoughts of freedom. Give a man a chance to get up there and he'll never be caught. The more desperate he is the more he'll do anything to have that chance, and the prospect of twenty years on the rock pile will make a man desperate.

Dusk and they're walking toward the prison gate, carrying cast-iron balls fixed to their ankles by chains, exhausted, slouching, coarse prison-striped, sweat-stained wool shirts and pantaloons clinging to their bodies. Guards armed with Henry rifles and shotguns stand along the way.

Chapman, talking low over his shoulder to Parsons, points out a wiry man with a pointy beard in the line ahead. "Name's Charlie Jones. We need him in with us. He's so mean and nasty I think he's got a screw loose. Killed a man over in White Pine; stabbed him in the heart. He'll take on anybody who comes after us." Chapman turns toward Parsons and thumps his chest in a stabbing motion.

Parsons, shoulders hunched, head sagging, trudges along behind Chapman. He left New Hampshire as a youngster when he shipped off to fight the rebels for Abe and the "Live Free or Die" state. The blown railroad job has him facing another nineteen years on the rock pile, so he's as likely to die as he is to live free.

Once a fancy gambler, time and wind and the fetid odor of the cell he calls home have gotten to him. His reddened eyeballs protrude and the lids stretch thin and opaque to cover them. He stops and scratches vigorously, angrily, at the sores on his arms caused by allergic reactions to his filthy uniform. "Goddamn it!"

Witching hour and the cell is bleak and black. Chapman is standing on his bunk punching the ceiling with a rag wrapped around his fist. The noise awakens his cellmate, eighteen-year-old J. B. Roberts, the youngest man in the prison.

"What's going on, Chapman?"

"It's hollow up there, just like I figured. Don't say anything to anybody or there'll be troubles. I'll talk to you about it in the morning."

The sun just coming up and they're already in the quarry, weary and still hungry after a breakfast of cold oatmeal and sludge-like coffee. Chapman leans over and whispers to Charlie Jones, who's bending down drinking from the ladle of a water bucket.

Jones, motionless, cocks his head and listens intently. With a crooked grin he tries to hide, he jerks upright. "Damn right I'm in. Just tell me when."

"Soon. Real soon."

Jones nods and slaps his thigh. "Yes," he hisses. "Yes."

2
"The Blow Would Be Heard the Fartherest By Any Mortal Man"

The reporter could hardly contain himself; it would be his greatest scoop. He telegraphed his newspaper that the blow would be heard "the fartherest by any mortal man."[1] He was standing by to describe to the nation the final blow of the ceremonial silver hammer that would drive the golden spike and complete the transcontinental railroad.

It was May 10, 1869. Locomotives of the Union Pacific Railroad coming from the east and the Central Pacific Railroad from the west were about to meet head-to-head at Promontory Summit in the Utah Territory just north of the Great Salt Lake. Not long after a war that had seen the deaths of over six hundred thousand at the hands of their countrymen, the nation was to become one again, at least symbolically.

Leland Stanford, the Central Pacific's president, would attempt the epochal blow in front of a raucous crowd of construction managers, politicians, Mormon leaders, newsmen, and railroad workers. He was one of the so-called Big Four entrepreneurs from Sacramento who had helped marshal the nation's economic forces to create the railroad from the Missouri to the Pacific. The circuits closed as the hammer was in its downward flight, and, even though Stanford missed the mark, wires went out to all corners of the country: "DONE."

The Central Pacific's wood-burning locomotive CPRR No. 60 (*Jupiter*) touched its pilot to that of the Union Pacific's coal-burner UPRR No. 119 to signal that the new, nation-expanding railroad was in operation.

Bret Harte, the editor of San Francisco's *Overland Monthly* literary journal, had just gained fame with "The Luck of Roaring Camp," his story about Thomas Luck, an orphan raised by miners in a small town in the Sierra foothills during the Gold Rush. The completion of the railroad inspired him to write of the international significance of the event:

---
[1] See Ambrose, *Nothing Like It in the World*, p. 366.

> What was it the engine said,
> Pilots touching—head to head
> Facing on the single track,
> Half a world behind each back?

Indeed there was half a world behind each back. It was, in combination with railroads built earlier in the East, the first railroad to across a continent.

In festivities that had begun a day earlier, bells tolled, locomotives whistled, and cannons roared across the land. It was the nation's heartiest celebration in the ninety-three years since John Adams had urged the celebration of the first Fourth of July by the ringing of bells and the release of fireworks. Parades in the cities were miles long; church doors opened; citizens would forever remember where they were when the news came. The Old Confederacy cheered as loudly as the North. Today, short of the celebrations that ended the world wars, it's difficult to imagine the joy, the pride, and, at last, the semblance of brotherhood.

Chicago's *Tribune* said the next day that the celebrations in that city were finally without the trappings of war "and the suggestions of suffering, danger and death which threw their oppressive shadow over the celebrations of our victories during the war for the union."

Just sixty-three years earlier, within the lifetimes of many who celebrated that day, Meriwether Lewis and William Clark and their intrepid band had completed a dangerous two-year trek to explore the recently purchased Louisiana Territory. President Thomas Jefferson had ordered them to prepare maps and send back samples of the biodiversity of the areas they traveled. They were also in search of a northwest passage he hoped would result in the economic unification of the east and west of the continent and, in a broader sense, the world. Now, with the completion of the railroad, people and goods would travel from east of the Mississippi to the Pacific Coast in less than a week. In effect it was the culmination of Jefferson's dream.

The transcontinental line—the Pacific Railroad as it was formally called—was the product of years of Congressional reports and hearings, shady financial sorties, lobbying activities that strained credulity, and marvelous feats of surveying, mapmaking, and engineering. In large part, however, it was brought about by the toil of countless laborers. The track was laid by European immigrant laborers, predominantly the Irish, working on the Union Pacific as it was built west, by Chinese immigrants working on the Central Pacific end of the line, by veterans of the Union and Confederate armies, and by Mormons who sought to have the route come near Salt Lake City.[2]

The completion of the railroad would change the face of America. In some cases, the changes were wholly unexpected.

The mines were in recession, and there was a manpower shortage in California in 1865. Difficulties encountered in crossing the Sierras had slowed construction of the Central Pacific line to the point that managers feared the Union Pacific would reach the Nevada-California border before the Central Pacific could even get over the mountains. Although there was resistance, the railroad began to hire unemployed Chinese miners and to recruit in China. The Chinese workers, who referred to themselves as "Celestials" after their homeland, the "Celestial Kingdom," proved so intelligent, hardworking, disciplined and adept that by the time Stanford hammered the golden spike, some eleven thousand Chinese laborers were at work. Their wages were twenty-six dollars per month (four dollars less than Caucasians), and they worked from sunrise to sunset. An unknown number died.

Irish laborers constructed portable hovels for living quarters as tracks were laid west from Omaha, sometimes at the rate of ten miles a day. The term "shantytown" came to be used in reference to these groups of plain-board shacks. ("Shanty" comes from the Gaelic *sean-tigh*, pronounced "shan tee," meaning "old house.") Railroad employment helped the Irish finally get into the mainstream workforce, as it did the Chinese.

Rail commerce would soon become directly involved in one of the country's defining controversies. In spite of the triumph of the Unionists in the war and the completion of the nation-spanning railroad, the country was not truly united.

---

[2] Mormon leader Brigham Young was a shareholder in the Union Pacific Railroad.

The Civil War Amendments to the Constitution abolished slavery and were meant to assure equal protection and due process of the law to all persons. The amendments notwithstanding, after Reconstruction ended and federal troops left the South, states there began to enact Jim Crow laws imposing systematic racial segregation. Louisiana enacted a statute (the Separate Car Act) requiring "separate but equal" accommodations for blacks and whites on intrastate railroads. In 1896, the United States Supreme Court ruled in the case of *Plessy v. Ferguson* that the railroad statute requiring separation of the races wasn't in violation of the Constitution, despite its obvious clash with the Fourteenth Amendment's equal protection clause.[3]

With the high court's endorsement, racial segregation proceeded unabated, fueled by the rise of the Ku Klux Klan and a sorry history of lynch mobs and oppression. This would assure that the nation would not begin the true process of unification for close to a century after the end of the Civil War.

Six decades after the *Plessy* decision, the Supreme Court's unanimous ruling in *Brown v. Board of Education* overturned it, spelling out why the notion of "separate but equal" when applied to races is "inherently unequal." Public railroad and other facilities could no longer be segregated. The civil rights movement and a succession of federal laws eventually put an end to segregation as a racial stratagem.

By the time the Pacific Railroad was completed, the fabled era of train robberies by familiarly named desperadoes had begun. Among those who pulled off daring robberies were Jesse and Frank James and the Younger brothers, whose exploits have been featured in so many fanciful Hollywood westerns.

---

[3] *Plessy* and the Dred Scott Decision of 1857 are generally acknowledged to be two of the worst US Supreme Court decisions of the nineteenth century. In *Dred Scott v. Sandford*, the court declared that black people of African ancestry, slaves as well as freemen, were not and could never be citizens; they were, in effect, personal property of their "owners" and could be bought and sold as merchandise. The decision also overruled the 1820 Missouri Compromise, thus permitting slavery in all the country's territories. President Lincoln's Emancipation Proclamation of 1863 and the Civil War Amendments to the Constitution (1865–1870) effectively nullified the decision.

Men being men, it was just a question of when and where robbers would hit the new transcontinental line. When the line was finally robbed, the men who did it followed a pattern set by the country's first train robbers in Indiana.

3
"Be Wary of the Thieves and Assassins That Infest the Place"

The Reno brothers found crime to their liking at early ages.

They grew up on a farm near Rockford, Jackson County, in south-central Indiana, not far from the little town of Seymour. Frank was born in 1837, John in 1838, and Sim in 1843. They had two younger brothers, William and Clinton, the latter being the only one who would avoid incarceration or early death.

The family was dysfunctional. The boys hated school and resented the strict religious training and compulsive Bible reading forced on them by their by-the-book ultrareligious parents, their father a Swiss emigrant and their mother Pennsylvania Dutch.

In 1858, the three older boys moved with their father to Seymour, where William eventually joined them. Frank Reno and his best friend, Frank Sparks, joined the Jackson County Volunteers in the Union army at the start of the Civil War but were discharged almost immediately. John Reno enlisted later but deserted.

Not inclined to work the farms, the brothers and Sparks found a clever, albeit dangerous, way of supporting themselves called "bounty jumping." Draftees who wanted to avoid service sought to hire men to take their places, and they were willing to pay handsomely. The boys signed up in the names of draftees, took their money, and promptly deserted. They also acted as brokers, finding substitutes and pocketing finders' fees. The risks they ran if caught were long prison terms, forced military service, and even execution.

As the war wound down and the economy with it, the Renos and Sparks brought together a motley bunch of sociopaths: bounty jumpers, counterfeiters and safe burglars, deserters and petty criminals. The group initially plundered in and around Rockford; their hideouts were burned-out buildings that were the result of the brothers' boyhood predations. As their area and mode of operations widened, post offices were robbed in Jonesville, Dudleytown, and Seymour; businesses were burgled; homes were invaded. The bar in the Rader House Hotel in Seymour eventually became the headquarters of the group, and there were regular reports of burglaries of guest rooms. Whoring, gambling, and drinking were daily pursuits.

One of the gang, Grant Wilson, was charged along with Frank Reno in the robbery of the Jonesville post office. Wilson turned state's evidence but was murdered before he could testify. Frank was released for lack of evidence; neither the robbery nor the murder was ever solved.

The citizenry lived in fear. Law enforcement was outmanned, its ranks decimated by the war. The criminal band was kept at arm's length by citizens afraid of retribution. According to accounts in archives of Pinkerton's National Detective Agency, the gang's "influence made itself felt even in local politics, corrupt officials being elected at the instigation of the outlaws; so that their [the outlaws'] convictions became practically impossible."

The youngest Reno sibling, Laura, didn't fall far from the family tree. She became known throughout the area for her beauty, love of danger and adventure, expertise as a horsewoman, and marksmanship. She was reputed to be as quick with a gun as any man. She was an outlaw version of Phoebe Ann Mosey (a.k.a. "Annie Oakley"), who would gain fame a few years later as a horsewoman and sharpshooter in Buffalo Bill's Wild West Show. One local newspaper said that Laura "fairly worshipped her desperado brothers, whom she aided in more than one of their criminal undertakings, shielding them from justice 'when [they were] hard-pressed,' and swearing to avenge them when retribution overtook them after their day of triumph."

The July 27, 1865, issue of the *Seymour Times* warned visitors to Jackson County to "be wary of the thieves and assassins that infest the place." A week later, an editorial declared with prescience that "nothing but Lynch law will save the reputation of this place and its citizens."

THE BACKDROP

In 1866, the head of a Rader House guest was found in the White River. More unsolved murders followed. When the Cortland post office was robbed, many locals thought they knew who the responsible parties were. Given the dearth of local law enforcement personnel, they sought help from the state legislature, but they were out of luck. Lawmakers were focused on the war and its aftereffects. In particular, there was intense statewide anger at the Copperheads, Southern sympathizers who opposed the Civil War and favored the reconstruction of a powerful new South. There was evidence that the Coppers were bringing in and illegally registering Kentucky residents to vote to elect pro-South legislators in Indiana. This social schism was what led to the strong Ku Klux Klan movement in the state.

Knowing they had the upper hand, the Renos and Sparks sought more lucrative criminal pursuits. The trains thundering by every day became objects of curiosity. They learned it was likely that military payroll was aboard as well as funds for banks and businesses along the line. They reckoned that more money was rolling by than was held by any business or post office within a hundred miles.

They watched and waited, connived and planned, from time to time pacing the trains rolling in and out of depots. They bought whiskey for workers as they sought intelligence on railroad operations.

On October 6, 1866, John and Sim Reno, Frank Sparks, and gang member Charles Gerroll boarded the Ohio and Mississippi train leaving Seymour. A few miles from town, they made their way to the Adams Express Company car, forced their way inside with crowbars, and at gunpoint disarmed and bound the lone clerk. They helped themselves to what company records described as "one safe the value of Thirty Dollars, Three Canvas Bags of the value of One Dollar Each, Ten Thousand Dollars in Gold coin and Thirty Three Dollars in Bank Notes."

Sim pulled the cord that signaled the engineer to halt the train. As it slowed, the other men shoved a safe out the door, and they all jumped. They were met by gang members with horses and a wagon.

The men held a drunken celebration that night at the Rader House. They probably had no idea that they had pulled off what would come to be recognized as the first successful train robbery in the country's history. Train robberies had been attempted earlier in the South, but the methodology and the large take of this particular incident gave widespread attention to this new type of crime. The gang came to be known as the country's first "Brotherhood of Outlaws."

Unknown to the robbers, the express car and its contents were under the protection of Chicago's Pinkerton Detective Agency. The agency, which provided security guard and crime-solving services, had been established by Allan Pinkerton in 1850. At one time it had more agents around the country than there were soldiers in the United States Army. The Pinkertons, as they were called, were occasionally hired to guard President Lincoln during the Civil War. Unfortunately they weren't there on his visit to Ford's Theatre.

Soon after the robbery, the Pinkertons located a witness, George Kinney, who had been aboard the train and could identify the robbers. The Renos and Frank Sparks were arrested but released on bail pending trial. A short time later, Kinney was cut down by gunfire when he answered a late-night knock at his door. Without a witness, prosecutors, who were none too anxious to proceed against the dangerous gang anyway, dropped the charges.

The release of the Renos and Sparks was followed by an unrelated (at least to prosecutors) gruesome rape and murder that put the people of Jackson County in a murderous uproar. They had had enough; the law apparently couldn't be enforced by elected officials or lawmen. The Jackson County chapter of the Secret Vigilance Committee of Southern Indiana vowed revenge. Also known as the Scarlet Mask Society, members either wore red bandanas over their faces or full hoods (like the knights of the KKK) when on the prowl.

Wary of the Society and its penchant for lynch parties, some of the gang members opted to leave the area. In a brazen act, they robbed the Daviess County Courthouse five hundred miles away in Gallatin, Missouri, of more than $20,000 dollars. John Reno was identified as one of the perpetrators. He was tracked down and, after a clever ruse, arrested by the Pinkertons in Seymour. The Scarlet Mask Society made an unsuccessful attempt to wrest him from jail. He was extradited to Missouri where he was tried, convicted, and sentenced to twenty-five years at hard labor in the state prison. He was paroled in 1878.

THE BACKDROP

After robbing several more government offices, Frank Reno and some of his cohorts were caught and jailed but managed to escape. Ignoring wanted posters proclaiming rewards for their capture dead or alive, they struck a train on May 23, 1868, outside Marshfield, just seventeen miles from the location of the first train robbery. They uncoupled the locomotive and express car, booted the engineer, and proceeded toward Seymour. The express clerk would not give them the keys to the safe, so as the train sped along in the middle of the night with Frank Reno at the throttle, they threw him out the door. Though seriously injured, he survived to provide details of the crime.

The heist netted the robbers a whopping $96,000 in bonds, cash, and currency, an unheard of amount for virtually any crime of the day. It didn't take the Pinkertons long to recognize that it was the handiwork of the Reno/Sparks gang. News of the crime was so widespread that several gang members headed for points north.

The less cautious among them, including Frank Sparks, stayed behind. On July 10, 1868, the gang stopped the Ohio & Mississippi train outside Brownstown, uncoupled the locomotive and express car, and roared off down the line. They did not get far before being stopped by a Pinkerton blockade. All but one of the robbers, a man named Volney Elliot, escaped after a shoot-out. Two, Charlie Rosenberry and Theodore Clifton, were identified by Elliot, tracked down, and locked in the Seymour jail. As Rosenberry, Clifton, and Elliot were being taken at night back to Brownstown to stand trial, a man waving a red lantern stopped the train and it was quickly surrounded by a masked mob. The three men were roughed up and unceremoniously hanged from the limb of a beech tree as the old German farmer who owned the property looked on bemused.

Frank Sparks and longtime gang members Henry Jerrell and John Moore were eventually captured and taken to Seymour. This time, the Pinkertons decided to move the prisoners to Brownstown in secret, but insiders discovered the move and put out the word.

Near where the first three men were strung up, masked men again stopped the train. Nooses were thrown over a tree branch, and the captives were made to stand on barrels. Jerrell and Moore sullenly refused to say anything. Sparks, however, "looked out over the

13

crowd with contemptuous bravado and, addressing them as a lot of 'mossback Hoosiers,' said he was glad he was not of their class and was proud to die a good Republican." The barrels were kicked away. The men didn't drop; the nooses tightened with their weight, and they slowly strangled. The spot between Seymour and Brownstown is still known as Hangman's Crossing.

The signs were ominous for the Reno brothers. The Pinkerton agency led an all-out effort to nab them. William and Sim were captured in Indianapolis, convicted of train robbery, and put inside a sturdy new jail in the town of New Albany in Floyd County to await relocation to the state penitentiary.

Meanwhile, Frank Reno had taken up residence in Windsor, Canada, where he partnered up with one Charles Anderson, a burglar, safe blower, and "short-card" gambler from England. Anderson had fled to the United States where he plied his various trades until the law got onto him.

Allan Pinkerton and an agent of one of the victimized railroad express companies located and procured the arrest of Reno and Anderson. Pinkerton sought permission of Canadian authorities to take them to Indiana. After a protracted extradition battle, they were released to his custody on the promise by United States authorities that they would be given a fair trial.

They were taken to the Floyd County jail to join William and Sim. The sheriff vowed that there was no danger vigilantes would get the four men: "They're here for safekeeping, and they'll be safely kept."

On the night of December 11, 1868, the Jefferson, Madison & Indianapolis train left the Seymour depot without lights or whistles, carrying some fifty men. After landing in New Albany, the men formed into columns led by a man called "Number One," who started the march to the jail with the words *salus populi suprema lex esto* (let the welfare of the people be the supreme law).[4]

Masked and hooded, they pounded on the jail door, yelling at full throat. When the jailer appeared he was overcome and shoved aside. The sheriff was shot in the arm as he set out to find help. Two county commissioners staying at the jail in anticipation of trouble

---

[4] The Latin phrase is on the great seal of the state of Missouri.

cowered in submission. Threatened with hanging, a jailer opened the door to the area where the prisoners were held.

Frank Reno was first on the death list. Ignoring his desperate protests, the vigilantes dragged the terrified man out of his cell, crammed a preknotted noose over his head, and threw the end of the rope over the rafters. The rope was yanked until his feet were just off the floor. After struggling for nearly two minutes, eyes bulging, face turning blue, he met his Maker.

William Reno, who was made to watch Frank die, was knotted up and suffered the fate of his brother. Right behind him was the Englishman Charles Anderson, crying, protesting, rightly so, that he had nothing to do with the Reno brothers' crimes. "My God, my God, this is a frame!"

Sim Reno fought hard but was beaten to a bloody pulp and strung up from a rafter in another corner of the jail. He watched, gurgling and gasping, as the bedlam faded. It took a quarter-hour for him to die.

Their business completed, the vigilantes locked the jail door. By prearrangement, they "hijacked" a train and ran it past the state prison near Jeffersonville before taking off in every direction. There were halfhearted investigations but no serious attempt to identify the perpetrators.

The newspaper that had prophesized the manner of the demise of the Reno brothers deftly summarized the events: "Judge Lynch has spoken."

Laura Reno, the lawless sister of the Reno boys who had once vowed revenge should they be harmed, seems to have gotten the message. She was not heard from again.

The exploits of the Reno/Sparks gang opened the door to a lengthy era of train robberies. The crimes became so common that newspapers used the melodramatic term "knights of the rail" in reference to the robbers, a term later used to describe train-hopping hoboes during the Great Depression.

Seven years after the first train robbery by the Renos and Sparks, the James/Younger gang infamously got into the act by tearing up the rails and causing the wreck of a Rock Island line train near Adair, Iowa, killing the engineer. The express car was robbed and the passengers, some gravely injured, were confronted by men in Ku Klux Klan regalia and relieved of their valuables. The robbers rode off to rebel yells.

Robert LeRoy Parker ("Butch Cassidy") and Harry Longabaugh (the "Sundance Kid") and their gang, dubbed the Wild Bunch by the press, went after railroads and banks. But by the time they pulled off the last major train robberies in the United States in Wyoming in 1899 and 1900, the Pinkertons, handsomely paid by the fed-up railroads, were out in force. Parker, Longabaugh, and his companion, Etta Place, sought refuge in South America, where they robbed banks to support themselves. Although the oft-told story is that the two men were killed in a shoot-out with Bolivian soldiers in 1908 and buried in the local cemetery, researchers have never found their remains. There is substantial evidence that they returned to the United States and lived under aliases for many years.

CHAPTER 2

The Railroad Comes West

1
Setting the Stage

The Spanish Franciscan missionary Fra Pedro Font, writing in his diary on June 29, 1776, described the scene as he looked northeast from a hill near where the Sacramento River empties into San Francisco Bay:

> We saw an immense treeless plain into which the water spreads widely, forming several small inlets; at the opposite end of this extensive plain, about forty leagues off, we saw a great snow-covered range [*una gran sierra Nevada*] which seemed to me to run from southeast to north north-west.

His map shows the upper portion of the Central Valley of California and to its east a mountain range running in the direction he described. "Sierra Nevada" translates variously as "snowy mountains" or "snow-capped peaks." His terminology was not unusual; it was a common descriptive phrase used by seventeenth- and eighteenth-century Spanish explorers and cartographers. What *is* unusual is that Fra Font's phrase stuck.

The day before the good father wrote that passage, Thomas Jefferson had submitted the Declaration of Independence to Congress in Philadelphia. The Declaration—effectively an act of war against England, the mightiest nation in the world—would be approved by the Continental Congress within a week. Twenty-seven years later, then president Jefferson would send Lewis and Clark and their men west on what would become the most famous expedition in his country's early history.

Fra Font had traveled north from Mexico on the second Anza expedition to explore Alta California. As he gazed at those peaks, he must have imagined they would forever be under the governorship of Spain. Yet, just three-quarters of a century later, the peaks and the land around him would become California, the thirty-first state of the United States. The mountains he named would be a formidable but final obstruction to an improbable and momentous engineering and construction feat that would bring together the far-flung outposts of a nation being created at the very moment Fra Font sat there awed at what he saw.

In his *California: A History*, Kevin Starr discusses the derivation of the name "California." Simply put, it is derived from myth.[1]

In 1510, the Spanish writer Garci Ordóñez de Montalvo published a romantic novel called *Las Sergas de Esplandian* (The Deeds of Esplandian). Widely read, the novel chronicled the imaginary exploits of Esplandian, son of Amadis of Gaul, at the siege of Constantinople. Among the allies of Esplandian were the Californians, a race of black amazons led by Queen Calafia. California, the tale went, was "an island on the right hand of the Indies ... very close to the side of the Terrestrial Paradise." It abounded in gold and precious stones.

Queen Calafia, whose amazons rode griffins into battle, was described as being large in person, young, beautiful and strong, and set on doing great things. She had sailed with her fleet to Constantinople to join in liberating the Holy Land. She ultimately became a Christian (of course), and the happy ending had her marrying one of Esplandian's officers.

The Spanish, Starr says, "had a tendency to conflate fact with fiction" when it came to prose romances like Montalvo's popular story. It comes as no surprise, then, that in 1533, Spanish conquistadores sailing west from Mexico under the command of Hernán Cortés landed on what they believed was the magical island described in the book. It was located, so they thought, in the recently discovered (from a European standpoint) Pacific Ocean near the East Indies. They named the island "California," hoping they would find there the riches Montalvo had described.

It would take six years from the first landing on the "island" for the explorers to discover their mistake. They were on a peninsula they came to call Baja California. North of the peninsula they found a broad region referred to on their maps as Antigua ("Old") California. Because of the financial and political circumstances of various Spanish kings and queens, the northern area would remain

---

[1] See Starr, pp. 5–6. See also Edward Everett Hale's article "The Queen of California," *Atlantic Monthly*, March 1864.

largely unexplored for another two centuries, by which time it would be referred to as Alta California. Fra Font was among the latter-day explorers.

There is general agreement that Montalvo formed the place-name "California" from the Spanish word *califa*, which was taken in turn from an Arabic word referring to the head of a caliphate. It is a legacy of some seven centuries of Moorish rule in parts of Spain that ended two decades before Montalvo wrote his novel.

In time, the Lewis and Clark expedition and others, including five led by John C. Fremont during the period 1842–54, would lead to the eventual settlement of Alta California and the West by the people of the new nation. Among the men who accompanied Fremont on some of his expeditions were those whose names decorate the maps of Nevada and California today, including Kit Carson, Joseph Walker, Edward Kern, and Richard Owens.[2] The maps that came out of the expeditions were widely published along with Fremont's notes. Drawn in large part by Fremont's German cartographer Charles Preuss, the maps were central to much of the mass migration westward.

On February 14, 1844, nearing the end of his second expedition, Fremont and Preuss climbed a peak at the Sierra crest (later named Red Lake Peak, it sits just north of Carson Pass) and were astonished to see a pristine lake ten or so miles to the north. Fremont judged the lake to be about fifteen miles long. It was the first known sighting of Lake Tahoe by nonindigenous people. A practical scientist himself, Fremont first named it Mountain Lake and then Lake Bonpland after the eminent French botanist Aime Jacques Alexandre Bonpland, who had accompanied early explorations of the Americas by German naturalist and explorer Friedrich Heinrich Alexander von Humboldt. The Humboldt River and Sink and Humboldt County in north-central Nevada and Humboldt Bay and County in northern California bear the latter's name.

---

[2] As a member of Fremont's third expedition, having been recommended to Fremont by Kit Carson, Dick Owens was among the first nonindigenous people to see the river and valley named after him by Fremont. They are in Inyo and Mono Counties in Eastern California. California's Kern County and the Kern River are named after Ed Kern, a topographer on the third expedition.

The foreign name "Bonpland" was not appealing to settlers, so the lake went through a series of names, including Lake Bigler, after California's third governor. Bigler, an outright secessionist and anti-Chinese bigot (he used the term "coolie" conversationally), was exceedingly unpopular after the Civil War; moreover Nevadans objected vociferously to calling the lake after a California governor. So the Indian name "Tahoe" gradually came into common use. Depending on one's sources, the name derives from the Washoe dialect "da aw" or "Da ow a ga" ("edge of lake" or "lake water") or from a Spanish word the Indians had picked up. The first use of "Tahoe" in government documents was by the Department of the Interior in 1862. In 1863 in one of his more famous sermons called "The Living Waters of Lake Tahoe," Reverend (and naturalist) Thomas Starr King asserted that the name derived from the Washoe "Tache" (Much Water) plus "Dao" (Deep or Blue Water). After a pro-longed two-state battle over what the lake should be called, and finally formally recognizing eighty years of history, the California legislature made "Tahoe" official from that state's standpoint in 1945. Nevadans had long since adopted the terminology. The twelve-by-twenty-mile lake straddles the Nevada-California border. Mount Starr King, named after the reverend, is a granite dome a few miles south of Half Dome in Yosemite National Park.

As if to give validity to California's island-of-gold founding myth, the discovery of gold in the Sierra foothills east of Sacramento in 1848, together with the enormous wealth and exploding population it engendered, would bring statehood two years later. The country's "manifest destiny," the term bandied about with increasing frequency by Senator Thomas Hart Benton (Fremont's father-in-law) and other expansionists in Congress now included faraway California.

This increased the political will to find a practical way to link the economies of the continent's east and west coasts. A railroad across the growing nation, until the Gold Rush little more than a dream, was just two decades from reality.

2
United by an Iron Roadway

For as long as the species has existed, humans have endeavored to move heavy loads from one place to another. A primitive wheelbarrow was perhaps the first successful labor-saving transport device constructed by the world's first inventor/engineer. The first "roads" would have been single-track paths cleared to make wheel dependent activities possible. The paths widened, people learned to use water and other media to compact surfaces, cobble stones came into use, and eventually Greek and Roman engineers learned to design and construct roads that were serviceable for centuries.

One of the early transport problems was to figure out how to construct surfaces smooth enough to avoid the expenditure of energy caused by uneven surfaces that resulted in inefficient vertical and side-to-side rather than directional movement. Another was how to best reduce the co-efficient of friction, which is the force that maintains contact between an object and a surface and the frictional force that resists the directional motion of the object. The solution: reduce the area of the contact of the object with the surface, smooth the surface itself, lessen the amount of non-directional movement, and the result is a lower co-efficient of friction, increased energy-efficient movement of the object, and lower cost. The perfect illustration of the concept is a flanged wheel moving on a smooth, narrow, strong surface; in other words, on the steel rail used on modern railroads.

Getting there took some time. The first tramways or "railroads" as they came to be called were constructed of round wooden rails—at first simply long, thin tree trunks (like juvenile lodge pole pines)—spiked down on wooden cross bars called "sleepers" (later "ties"). Eventually the "rails" were sawn and capped with hardwood or plates of iron. The term "platelayer" is still used on occasion in England to denote workers who fix rails to ties. Derailments as loads shifted or roadbeds tilted were common occurrences despite attempts to fashion some sort of wheel with a central groove. It wasn't until 1789 that William Jessup designed the first railway wagon with flanged wheels to prevent side-slip.

An important early use of rails came in England about 1630 when a coal mine proprietor in Northumberland named Beaumont, who had built wagon roads by using heavy planks for horses to pull carts, hit on the idea of fixing plated rails to the planks. In order to prevent the rails from spreading, he soon learned to anchor the rails to sleepers, which were in turn fixed to the planks. Although he wasn't the first coal producer to try this, Mr. Beaumont it appears had constructed the first efficient commercial railway. The locomotive force remained the horse.

Scotsman James Watt built the first modern stationary steam engine in 1774. Inventive minds immediately began to think about how to harness steam power to wagons.

Toward the end of the eighteenth century, American inventor Oliver Evans, following along the lines of experimenters in England, worked up plans to apply steam power to a common horse carriage. In 1800 he predicted that the "time will come when people will travel in stages moved by steam engines from one city to another, as fast as birds can fly, 15 or 20 miles an hour…A carriage will start from Washington in the morning, the passengers will breakfast at Baltimore, dine at Philadelphia, and sup in New York the same day." Whether he was thinking of a carriage moving on a road like a wagon or on rails is not certain. What is certain, as subsequent events bore out, is that he was on the right track (so to speak).

Aware of the work of Evans and others, the ever-prescient Jefferson said in 1802 that the "introduction of so powerful an agent as steam [to a carriage on wheels] will make a great change in the situation of man." That the changes he anticipated would transform his country so rapidly would have astonished even the scientific minded Jefferson. When he made that statement the Louisiana Purchase was in the talking stages, Lewis and Clark had yet to begin preparations for their epic journey, and the dimensions and topography of lands west of the Mississippi were largely unknown. Yet just 67 years later locomotives would cross the continent in a matter of days.

In 1804 Englishman Matthew Murray invented a steam locomotive that ran on timber rails. In 1807 the first passenger train ran from

Swansea to Mumbles. The era of railroads in the modern sense was under way. Rapid improvements in the science of metallurgy and in tool-making would give impetus to railroad development. Various engine and rail designs were tried over the next two decades, largely in England, and steady improvements ensued.

A steam locomotive capable of efficiently and economically hauling large numbers of passengers or considerable freight tonnage, the *Rocket*, was built by George and Robert Stephenson at Newcastle Upon Tyne in 1829 and served the Liverpool & Manchester Railway. The locomotive, the finest of its day, could haul 30 passengers at a remarkable 30 miles per hour. It was remarkable in large part because it was much faster than a horse could pull a carriage, thus assuring that the happy horse would soon find its way out of cities and towns and back to the country's bucolic byways.

In 1829 Peter Cooper of New York built the *Tom Thumb*, a primitive locomotive that hauled a few passengers on the Baltimore and Ohio Railroad. The B & O was the first rail line built in a westerly direction, from Baltimore to the Ohio River. Before Cooper's locomotive came along the B & O had experimented with windpower (sails on a carriage) and had utilized horses to draw vehicles along its rails. Given this interwoven development, it is little wonder that "horsepower" became the accepted term to gauge the comparative power of steam locomotives and, later, gasoline engines.

The first commercially successful, completely American-built steam engine to go into scheduled passenger service, beginning in 1830, was the *Best Friend of Charleston*. It was followed by the *DeWitt Clinton* in 1831.

In the early days as railroads were constructed in the East and Midwest, technological problems assured that the construction of a transcontinental line would remain a dream, at least for a while. Track was poorly laid; braking devices were primitive; fatal accidents were common. Passenger carriages came with wood or coal-burning stoves and oil lamps for illumination, a certain danger on trains lurching about on irregular tracks.[3] Engines spewed so much smoke that tracks were routed to assure that the poorest parts of towns would be on the downwind side, or "the wrong side of the tracks."

---
[3] Fire was a danger for decades. For example, in 1921 twenty-seven passengers were killed in a stove fire on a train outside Philadelphia.

A primary cause of danger was that tracks and engine boilers were made of cast iron, which had a tendency to fail under tension or pressure. Rails worked loose, cracked, and buckled under the strain of heavy traffic. Cast-iron railway boilers often exploded; in fact, the boiler of the *Best Friend of Charleston* exploded just a year after it was put into operation, killing its fireman.

In 1856 the metallurgy problem was solved somewhat unexpectedly by the Englishman Henry Bessemer, an inventor who had decided to experiment with blowing air into molten pig iron. Instead of the explosion naysayers predicted, the process created a flame of high intensity that burned out impurities in the iron. What became the Bessemer converter was a fast and efficient way to produce steel. Steel was not unknown, but it had been too expensive to produce to be of widespread value. Thanks to Bessemer, virtually anything required to withstand significant weight and pressure, including boilers, train tracks, and railway bridges, could be built stronger and cheaper.

By 1860, more than thirty thousand miles of track linked the cities and farmlands of the East and Midwest. This growth was significantly boosted, beginning in the 1880s, by Andrew Carnegie, who amassed his fortune in large part by improving on Bessemer's technology in the cheap, efficient mass production of steel rails and bridges.

Well before the advent of these technologies, entrepreneurs, politicians, and financiers recognized that a transcontinental railroad would in time be practical and would facilitate enormous economic growth. With the application of innovative engineering techniques, it would be possible to build rail lines through and across the rivers, canyons, and mountain ranges of the vast American West. A practicable route, financing, and leadership were needed.

As early as 1819 when railway technology was still in its formative states, Robert Mills, a friend of Thomas Jefferson, proposed a "steam carriage" to run from the Mississippi to the Columbia. Mills was the architect of the Washington Monument and other federal buildings. Despite his standing and connections, with Jefferson largely out of the picture his idea was studiously ignored in power circles. But it caught on elsewhere.

In 1832 Samuel Dexter, the editor of the *Western Emigrant* of Ann Arbor, Michigan, wrote a well received editorial detailing a plan "to unite New-York and the Oregon by a railway" that would transport its passengers at the rate of ten miles an hour. As rail construction and traffic grew, the nation came alive with editors and writers touting the economic boost a transcontinental line would give the country. In accord with an elementary law of nature, when the public takes notice, politicians are sure to embrace an idea in due time.

Perhaps the most important of the early transcontinental-line visionaries was Asa Whitney, born in Connecticut in 1797. A distant cousin of Eli Whitney, the inventor of the cotton gin, he was a merchant who married into the family of John Jay, the first chief justice of the Unites States and later governor of New York. After a series of business misfortunes and the death of his wife, Whitney departed for China in 1842 to study the commercial possibilities of trade with that country. A good businessman and practical man, a sharp observer of matters economic, he prospered in businesses related to the exportation of teas, spices and other Asian goods. On his return to America two years later, financially secure for life, he vowed to use his energies to do something good for mankind: he would see to it that a locomotive would travel to the shores of the Pacific and thereby increase trade with Asia many times over.

Whitney had seen George Stephenson's *Rocket* in 1830 and had ridden at then exceptional speeds on the Liverpool and Manchester Railroad. The link in his mind between the railroad, the Pacific, and Asia was thus no sudden light bulb of an idea. And on returning from China he fortuitously stepped back into a country fervent with the notion of expansion: into Texas, and to the Rockies, California, and Oregon.

Whitney set about writing a detailed paper—a 'memorial' he called it—advocating as immediately practicable the construction of a railroad from Michigan to the Pacific Ocean. He argued that the economic benefits of such a project would be incalculable. Congressman Zadock Pratt of New York read the paper into the record of the House of Representatives in 1845 and was later an author of the legislation that directed the secretary of war to survey five potential rail routes to the West Coast. The paper was referred to committee and congressional consideration of a transcontinental railroad was underway, however sporadic it would come to be over the next nearly two decades.

After tirelessly traveling the country to promote his idea, Whitney gradually faded from sight after the House ignored his impassioned pleas for railway surveys and funding at a special session in 1851. He died of typhoid fever in 1872. Nonetheless, his efforts eventually proved fruitful, carried forth by another man who saw the future. Theodore Judah would come into the picture shortly after Whitney had his problems with Congress.

Abraham Lincoln was born on February 12, 1809,[4] three months before the end of Jefferson's second presidential term and just thirty-three years after the Spanish priest/explorer Fra Pedro Font, writing in his journal near San Francisco Bay, described the Sierra Nevada. As a young Illinois lawyer running for the legislature, Lincoln said in 1832, in promoting a railroad line from the Illinois River to Springfield, that "no other improvement ... can equal in utility the rail road" for the good of the nation's commerce.

Although not elected to office on that first try, Lincoln continued to promote railroad construction and commerce throughout his life. He argued in favor of government financing for construction and opined on the proper regulation of rail commerce. Among the nation's first and finest railroad lawyers, he litigated several cases that set favorable precedents for railroads, one of which established that railroads were as important as rivers for commerce (*Hurd v. Rock Island Bridge Company*, the so-called *Effie Afton* case).

In a case involving the taxation of railroads, *Illinois Central Railroad Company v. McLean County*, Lincoln prevailed in the Illinois Supreme Court, thereby saving his client millions. But the railroad refused to pay his fee, saying it was as much as the great Daniel Webster himself would have charged.[5] Lincoln brought suit and was awarded more than double his original billing. The railroad cut its losses by wisely keeping the young lawyer on retainer.

---

[4] Charles Darwin was born the same day in Shrewsbury, England.
[5] Donald, *Lincoln*, p. 156. Daniel Webster (1782–1852) of Massachusetts was a legendary lawyer, orator, and abolitionist. Along with lawyers Henry Clay (1777–1852) of Kentucky, a moderate, and John Calhoun (1782–1850) of South Carolina, a vehement defender of slavery, Webster figured prominently in the defining political battles in the United States Senate leading to the Civil War.

The country had railroad fever, although it abated somewhat as the country's attention and resources were directed to the Mexican War. But with California gaining statehood in 1850 and with it the securing of the Pacific Coast against Spanish, British, and Russian pretenders, the push for a transcontinental line reemerged with increased fervor.

In 1853, finally realizing the wisdom of visionary Asa Whitney, Congress called for a survey of potential cross-country rail routes. Jefferson Davis, the secretary of war, sent surveyors to search out five alternative routes to the West Coast, ranging from a northern route close to Canada to a southern route near Mexico. The surveyors' reports gave the most complete picture of the West yet developed. Davis, soon to become president of the Confederate States of America, argued for the southern route from Texas to San Diego, but no Northern politician would approve a route that had the potential to extend slavery. On the other hand, slave-state politicians were as vigorously opposed to routes that would head west from Chicago, Saint Louis, and Minneapolis. Congressional activities ground to a halt. The logjam would be broken only when the Southern states seceded, leaving a Congress of Northerners and an anti-slavery president to pick a route.

Lincoln took office as the sixteenth president of the United States in March 1861. He immediately urged Congress to act on a transcontinental railroad bill, and he 1never let up. After nearly continuous House and Senate Committee hearings, intense lobbying, and emotionally charged debates over the route the railroad would take, how it would be financed, and who would build it, Congress enacted the Pacific Railway Act; it became law when signed by Lincoln on July 1, 1862.

The bill created the Union Pacific Railroad to construct the line west from the Missouri, while California's Central Pacific Railroad would build east from Sacramento. Among the more important provisions of the legislation were federal financial guarantees to assure sufficient private investment in the venture. An amendment in 1864 strengthened the financial guaranties and provided substantially more benefits to the railroad companies in the form of land grants.

A controversy soon erupted over where westward construction should begin. It was obvious that land along the route would greatly increase in value, so speculators, the nearly broke John C. Fremont among them, used every lobbying tactic available, including bribery, to have construction begin near or pass through lands in which they had interests. Prevailed upon by Union general Grenville Dodge, Lincoln ended what could have become a ruinous political controversy by issuing an executive order making clear that westward construction would start at Omaha. The order was issued on November 17, 1863, two days before the Gettysburg Address.

Lincoln had met Grenville Dodge, then a twenty-eight-year-old civil engineering graduate of a Vermont military academy, in 1859. The meeting took place at Council Bluffs, Iowa, a settlement on the western boundary of the state across the Missouri River from Omaha. It was the anchor point for several immigrant trails.[6] Lincoln had learned that Dodge had done detailed studies of potential rail routes to the Pacific. Pressed by trial lawyer Lincoln's questions, Dodge demonstrated why the optimal route was west from Omaha, roughly along the forty-second parallel through the Platte Valley, the Rocky Mountains, and on to points west. In recalling the meeting, Dodge wrote, "Mr. Lincoln sat down beside me and, by his kindly ways, soon drew from me all I knew of the country west and the results of my reconnaissances. As the saying is, he completely 'shelled my woods,' getting all the secrets that were later to go to my employers."

The young engineer so impressed Lincoln that he advocated the Dodge route as the railroad legislation wound through Congress. He heeded Dodge's advice again in 1863 when he issued his executive order establishing the starting point for westward construction.

After that first meeting with Lincoln, Dodge went on to distinguish himself in battle in the Civil War. Attaining the rank of general, he became a confidant of generals Ulysses S. Grant, William T. Sherman, and John S. Casement, among other high ranking military commanders. In the years after Lincoln's death, they would assist Dodge as he successfully battled with managers

---

[6] Lincoln lost the 1858 race for US senator from Illinois to Stephen Douglas, but his political reputation was on the rise, in part because of his seven famous debates with Douglas. He would win the Republican nomination for president the year after he met Dodge. Council Bluffs is so named because it was the site of a meeting between Lewis and Clark and leaders of the Otoe Tribe in 1804.

of the Union Pacific who interfered with his efforts and those of the other principal engineer, Samuel B. Reed, to complete the Union Pacific line.

Another young engineer—a first-rank American visionary—would play the principal role in the Central Pacific's construction of the transcontinental line east from Sacramento. Born in 1826 in Connecticut, Theodore Judah studied engineering at Rensselaer Polytechnic Institute. After working on railroads in the east, he was hired in 1853 as chief engineer for the Sacramento Valley Railroad, the first railroad constructed west of the Mississippi. William T. Sherman was in the group that financed and managed the railroad for the purpose of serving California's gold country. Sherman had resigned his army commission to move west to assume the vice presidency of the railroad. Achieving little success in the railroad business, he sold his interests, became a schoolmaster in Louisiana, and finally reenlisted and gained fame for his exploits during the Civil War.

Soon after reaching Sacramento, Judah began studying routes and advocating the seemingly impossible construction of a rail line over the Sierras—in other words, the initial step in what he knew would become the first railroad to cross a continent, a thought had been on his mind even before he ventured west. He wrote a pamphlet called *A Practical Plan for Building the Pacific Railroad* and distributed it to politicians in Washington DC and Sacramento in early 1857. It evoked interest in Congress, but regional jealousies over the route's location precluded significant action. The *Practical Plan* promoted a route from the Platte Valley to Sacramento similar to the one that Glenville Dodge would pitch to Abraham Lincoln two and a half years later.

Judah's plan astonished many and earned him the nickname Crazy Judah. He had the audacity to predict that in time trains powered by enormous locomotives with driving wheels fourteen feet in diameter would cross the continent in less than two days. Undeterred, he pressed on.

In 1859, the California legislature set up a convention in San Francisco for the purpose of promoting a Pacific railroad. The result, at Judah's urging, was a resolution calling for Congress to establish a central railroad route to Sacramento and provide a way to finance it. Judah was selected to take the matter to Washington.

Faced with legislators skeptical that a railroad could ever cross the Sierras, Judah returned to California and set out to prove them wrong. After examining and rejecting several possible routes through the mountains, he was contacted by Daniel W. "Doc" Strong, a druggist from the Sierra placer mining town of Dutch Flat. Strong took him on a ride east along an old immigrant trail that crossed the mountains at Donner Pass and dropped a thousand feet down to Donner Lake. The trail was marked by slashes on trees made by the Donner Party and their rescuers in 1847. Judah quickly realized that a rail line could be constructed along the trail and that the steep grade from the pass to the lake could be managed. He would eventually ride farther east from Donner Lake, down the Truckee River Canyon, and out into Nevada. The mountains were passable, and he had his route at last. His luck took a good turn when railroad advocate Lincoln was elected president just about the time Judah returned to Washington.

Judah was such an effective lobbyist for the railroad cause that he was given an office in the Capitol, which he turned into a railroad museum. Respected by legislators for his knowledge and energy, he was appointed secretary of the Senate Pacific Railroad Committee and was a clerk for a House subcommittee on the Pacific Railroad. His work was more instrumental than that of any other person, except perhaps Lincoln, in securing passage of the railroad bill. It was said that on its passage he immediately sent a wire to the Central Pacific office at 54 K Street in Sacramento: "We have drawn the elephant. Now let us see if we can harness him up."[7]

Earlier when in California, Judah had drawn up the articles of incorporation for what would eventually be the Central Pacific Railroad. Faced with financial difficulties and lacking funds for a survey of his transmountain route, he convened a group of Sacramento businessmen to secure their backing. Four of them who were otherwise ordinary merchants—Leland Stanford (groceries), Charles Crocker (dry goods), and Collis P. Huntington and Mark Hopkins (partners in a hardware business)—proved to be superb politicians and fundraisers. Eventually calling themselves "the Associates," they

---

[7] See Bain at p. 115 and authorities there cited.

were leaders in Lincoln's fledgling Republican Party in California. They ran for political offices (Stanford served a term as governor), lobbied Congress, and raised the funds for a survey by Judah of his newfound route through the mountains. The survey became the linchpin for Congressional action.

The Associates had the good judgment to keep Judah in the picture as the Central Pacific's chief engineer, but as matters progressed, they began to edge him out. His trouble stemmed in large part from the fact that as a member of the nominating committee he had recommended Stanford rather than Huntington to be president of the Central Pacific. The powerful, overtly political Huntington never got over it.

Judah had an option to purchase the company for $400,000. Recognizing his problems with the Associates, he sat out for the east coast to raise the money. In an abrupt turn of luck, he contracted yellow fever while crossing the Isthmus of Panama and died four months later in New York at age thirty-eight. Thus the man who was responsible more than any other for the success of the Central Pacific did not live to enjoy the fame and reap the benefits he deserved.

Now with complete control, the Associates awarded the contract for the construction of the railroad to a dummy corporation they owned. In January 1863, while he was serving as governor, Stanford broke ground for the construction of the Central Pacific line from Sacramento, over the Sierras along the route Judah had surveyed, down the Truckee River Canyon, and through Nevada to its linkup with the Union Pacific line somewhere east, depending on the relative speeds at which the Central and Union lines could be constructed. Stanford wielded the hammer to pound the final spike when the railroads met in the Utah Territory six years later.

As a result of land grants provided by Congress in the railroad bill, the Central Pacific, its shareholders, and its successors would rank among the largest landowners and richest corporations in the country. Thanks to the late Theodore Judah, the Associates, who once held forth from humble storefronts on J and K Streets in Sacramento, would reap fortunes exceeding $200 million.

Stanford declined a second term as governor, preferring to serve as president of the Central Pacific Railroad. The railroad and its successors gained such complete control of the California legislature—its lobbyists calling the shots on budgets and anything else that might affect the railroad's operations and land holdings—that several decades later Governor Hiram Johnson ran on an anti-railroad platform and led a successful effort to amend the state constitution in order to dilute the railroad's influence. The amendments, including initiative and referendum procedures by which the public could enact its own laws or override the legislature, gave California a degree of democracy untouched by any other state.

Had he lived to see the completion of the Pacific Railroad, Lincoln almost certainly would have been at Promontory Summit to hammer the final spike. It is also likely that he'd have been involved with railroads in a major way after his presidency and that he'd have prospered in such an endeavor. The loss to the country by his assassination at a relatively young age can only be imagined. Ironically and fittingly, the people followed and mourned as his cortege stretched seventeen hundred miles over fourteen days along the tracks of fourteen railroads from Washington DC to his resting place in Oak Ridge Cemetery in Springfield, Illinois.

The Governor Stanford locomotive entered service in 1863 and was used in constructing the Central Pacific portion of the transcontinental railroad. (Courtesy of Nevada Historical Society)

May 10th, 1869, Promontory Point, Utah Territory, Central Pacific president Leland Stanford prepares to use the Silver Hammer to drive the Golden Spike and complete the transcontinental railroad. (Courtesy of Nevada Historical Society)

3
Hard Country

When Congress was considering the railroads bills, Reno had yet to acquire its name. The tiny settlement in the Truckee Meadows adjacent to the Truckee River[8] was called Lake's Crossing. Truckee was a Paiute chief who had provided guidance and assistance to Fremont's second expedition and to early westward-bound immigrants facing the daunting challenge of a Sierra crossing. The dangers of crossing the mountains was dramatically borne out by

---

[8] John Fremont called it the Salmon Trout River. The Paiutes at Pyramid Lake, the terminus of the river, had fed his starving party on the large, abundant, salmon-like lake and river trout. Fremont also named the lake, a rock formation protruding from it reminding him of the Great Pyramid of Giza.

the privations of the Donner Party, marooned by heavy snowfall at the foot of today's Donner Pass in the winter of 1846/47.

The settlement on the Truckee was described by one writer as being "nothing more than a connection between the Comstock and the outer world." Comstock was a reference to the Comstock Lode, a silver discovery in 1858 near Virginia City, then a scruffy mining town twenty miles to the south of incipient Reno on the eastern slopes of Mount Davidson near the southern end of the Flowery Range.

When word got out of the discovery by prospectors Peter O'Riley and Patrick McLaughlin of fabulously rich silver veins coursing through the mountain, the population exploded. Virginia City quickly became the most populous city in what was soon to become the state of Nevada.[9] It was the richest mineral strike in the country's history, yielding some $400 million in gold and silver ore through 1878 (billions in today's dollars).

The lode's namesake, Henry "Old Pancake" Comstock, was an obscure prospector who had been rooting around in the area. How he did it is a mystery—strong drink is a ready suspect—but he convinced Riley and McLaughlin that he had already staked the area where they made their claim. The dispute was settled when he bought them out for forty dollars cash, a bottle of whiskey, and a blind horse.[10] Although he'd have soon been worth millions, Comstock sold his interests for $10,000. He died in Montana in 1870, a penniless suicide battling the onset of dementia.

Some thirty thousand people converged on the area. In a reverse migration called the "Rush to Washoe," many returned east over the mountains after failing to strike it rich in California's gold rush. Among them was a man named Pleasant Arthur Chalfant—an original 49er—about whom more is told later as this story approaches its end.

---

[9] It was then part of the Utah Territory. A substantial majority of the citizens of Virginia City and Carson City had grown tired of being governed from a distance of six hundred miles by Brigham Young, a person they considered to be a religious tyrant. Apart from the nationwide controversy over slavery, separation from Utah was the hottest local political issue of the day. The act creating the Nevada Territory was signed by President James Buchanan on March 2, 1861, two days before he was succeeded by Abraham Lincoln.

[10] Morris Jr., p. 69.

James "Old Virginny" Finney was a hard-up prospector who had made his way west from Virginia. In 1850, well before the silver bonanza, he and three other men struck gold in the area and made enough to keep themselves in food and drink. Finney was a well-known character who enjoyed his booze. Legend has it that while drunk in his favorite watering hole one night he dropped a half-full bottle of whiskey. Fearful lest his beloved thirst quencher be wasted, he decided to use it for ceremonial purposes. He stomped on the floor boards where the bottle had broken and shouted to the assembled imbibers, "I christen this place Virginia City!"

Finney died in 1861 after being thrown from a horse while drunk. Like most prospectors, he had hardly a penny to his name.

Life in Virginia City and other mining camps scattered around Nevada and the Mother Lode was primitive and dangerous. Mining itself wreaked havoc in the eyes of some. Noted travel writer John Ross Browne described the basics of mining in self-professed horror.

> Myriads of swarthy, bearded, dust-covered men are piercing into the grim old mountains, ripping them open, thrusting murderous holes through the naked bodies; piling up engines to cut their vital arteries; stamping and crushing up with infernal machines their disemboweled fragments, and holding fiendish revels amid the chaos of destruction.[11]

Guns were ubiquitous. Referring to his days on the Comstock, Mark Twain remarked that he wore a holstered pistol so as not to be "offensively conspicuous, and a subject of remark."[12] He described Virginia City as only he could.

> Money was as plenty as dust; every individual considered himself wealthy, and a melancholy countenance was nowhere to be seen. There were military companies, fire companies, brass bands, banks, hotels, theaters, "hurdy-

---
[11] Mack, p. 185.
[12] Twain, p. 153.

gurdy houses," wide-open gambling palaces, political pow-wows, civic processions, street fights, murders, inquests, riots, a whiskey mill every fifteen steps, a Board of Aldermen, a Mayor, a City Surveyor, a City Engineer, a Chief of the Fire Department, with First, Second and Third Assistants, a Chief of Police, City Marshal and a large police force, two Boards of Mining Brokers, a dozen breweries and a half a dozen jails and station-houses in full operation, and some talk of building a church.[13]

When a man wasn't mining or wrangling, he was probably bored, and that was conducive to fighting. "What is there to do in this town, anyway?" a cowboy asked Canby. "You have five choices," Canby replied. "Eat, sleep, drink, play poker, or fight. Or you can shoot some pool." Canby owned a saloon in fictional Bridger's Wells in Nevadan Walter Van Tilburg Clark's classic Western novel *The Ox-Bow Incident*, set in Nevada in 1885. (Published in 1940, the novel was adapted to film. The much-acclaimed movie starred Henry Fonda and Harry Morgan.)

Women were few, so a man's prospects were bleak. Rose Mapen was run out of Bridger's Wells by the few married women there, who considered her to be an unsavory character. After that, the only single woman in town Canby knew was "eighty-two, blind, and a Piute."

The robbery of stagecoaches and freight wagons was a lucrative profession for men daring enough to do it. They were popularly referred to as "road agents." Although guards known as "shotgun messengers" often rode stages alongside the teamster, that didn't slow robbers much in the early days. A stage driver from San Francisco who was plying his trade in the mining camps around Aurora, Nevada, commented:

> Until you have been suddenly called upon to look down the opening of a double-barreled shotgun, which has a road agent with his hand on the trigger at the other end, you can have no idea how surprised you are capable of

---
[13] Id. at p. 157.

being. I have had a six-shooter pulled on me across a faro table; I have proved that the hilt of a dirk can't go between two of my ribs; I have seen four aces beaten by a royal flush; but I was never really surprised until I looked down the muzzle of a shotgun in the hands of a road agent. Why, my friend, the mouth of the Sutro tunnel is like a nail-hole in the Palace Hotel compared to a shotgun.[14]

The Sutro Tunnel referenced in the quote was completed in 1878. It was one of several on the Comstock constructed to draw water from inside the mountains, provide better ventilation, and thereby allow access for deeper mineral exploration. It begins at Virginia City and ends six miles down through the mountain near Dayton.

The Palace Hotel was constructed in 1875, destroyed in the 1906 San Francisco earthquake, and rebuilt in 1909. When first constructed it was reputed to be the largest, most luxurious, and costliest hotel in the world. According to the hotel's web site, many presidents have stayed there. Warren G. Harding died in 1923 in room 8064. The hotel houses perhaps the most famous bar in the West, The Pied Piper, which is named after Maxfield Parrish's 1909 painting of the same name. The painting hangs behind the bar.

Thompson and West's 1881 *History of Nevada* reported that there were over four hundred known homicides shortly before and after Nevada became a state. Most were the result of drink and reckless bravado and were carried out to prove one's manhood. "Persons meet in saloons, bagnios and gambling places with deadly weapons upon their persons; they drink, gamble, dispute when half intoxicated, banter each other, and at last draw out their weapons for fancied causes alone and slay each other."[15]

Details of a few of the homicides provide a picture of the dangers of life on the frontier:

---

[14] *Bodie Standard*, July 20, 1871
[15] See Thompson and West at p. 341, et. seq.

The first killing mentioned in the *History* occurred on October 5, 1846, at Gravelly Ford along the Humboldt Trail in what is now east-central Nevada. It wasn't the result of drink; rather, James F. Reed, a leader of what history now calls the Donner Party, intervened in a dispute between two teamsters. One of them, John Snyder, was so enraged that when Reed tried to stop the fight, Snyder struck him in the face with a bullwhip. Reed pulled a knife and killed Snyder. After considering hanging him, the other party leaders decided to send Reed ahead to Sacramento for supplies. It was, so they thought, the equivalent of a death sentence.

Reed reached Sutter's Fort in Sacramento on October 28, 1846, just three weeks after being banished. He had crossed some four hundred miles of mountains and deserts, the likes of which he'd never seen. An early snowfall prevented his crossing back over the Sierras with supplies. With Sutter's people, he got caught up in the Mexican-American War and fought in the Battle of Santa Clara in January 1847. He returned to Sutter's Fort in February. Surprised that his family was not there, he surmised they were trapped in the Sierras and organized a search party. The last living, bedraggled, starving members of the Donner party were found and guided safely down through the deep snows and across the roaring rivers of the western slopes of the mountains.

Reed became a prosperous merchant in San Jose and a leader in California's march to statehood. A few of his effects remain on display in Sutter's Fort. The story of the acts of cannibalism by some members of the Donner Party, none involving Reed's family, is well known.

In 1861, a man named McKenzie was killed by Sam Brown in Virginia City. "Brown ran a knife into his victim, and then turned it around, completely cutting the heart out, then wiped his bloody knife and laid [sic] down on a billiard table and went to sleep."

Brown was a Texas-born bad man, a man to fear when drunk. Using his favorite weapon, the bowie knife, he had reputedly left sixteen victims in his wake in Texas, California, and Nevada. When he threatened to make Genoa resident Henry Van Sickle the next in line, the alert Van Sickle got the jump with a bullet to Sam's body; he added seven more to the head and torso just to make sure Sam and his knife were down for the count. A coroner's jury exonerated

Van Sickle, finding that Brown had died "from a just dispensation of an all-wise Providence."[16]

In 1863 in Virginia City, Charles Seeger was shot and killed by Deborah Ann Phillips for using insulting language. She was sentenced to a year in prison, but she was quickly pardoned by Nevada's territorial governor James W. Nye, a shrewd New York City politician appointed by Abe Lincoln. Soon to become the state's first governor, he apparently had a soft spot for distressed damsels, even if women couldn't vote.

In May 1868 in Austin, Lander County, Noble Slocum was killed by young Rufus Anderson, who was sentenced to be hung on October 29. "The noose not being properly fastened slipped as the trap was sprung, and the doomed boy landed on the ground upon his feet. This was repeated, and the excited crowd began to think of rescuing him. But upon the third attempt, strangulation was completed."

In April 1872, James Fund was killed in Eureka by his wife, Hattie: "Cause, domestic infelicity, and too much whiskey." Hattie wasn't charged, reflecting Nevada's concern for women who dared the frontier.

Later that year, George Kirk was hanged by vigilantes. "He had been ordered to leave town, and came back; was found drunk in a dance-house, taken to the Sierra Nevada works and hung; had '601' painted on him." Vigilantes often pinned numbers on their victims, the significance of the numbers depending on the whims of the executioners.

James Donovan was shot and killed by Frank Killet in a mining camp in Nye County in December of 1876. "The men agreed to settle a dispute with pistols and were to walk twenty-five steps in opposite directions and then commence firing. Donovan proved treacherous and turned at seventeen steps. His pistol missed fire, when Killet shot him dead. The Grand Jury refused to indict him."

In October 1877, Andrew Mills and a Mr. Redell got into a fatal tiff in Tuscarora, Elko County. "An old grudge existed between the parties for a long time. Mills struck Redell with an ax, and killed

---

[16] Morris Jr., p. 110.

him, after he was shot by the latter. Both died." The townsfolk generally agreed that the double deaths precluded a trial and thereby saved the county a pile of money.

S. E. Merrill was killed by Mattias Salmon in Greenville, Nye County. "The murderer was hanged to a windmill on the same night by 'vigilantes' with '329' pinned on him. Salmon is said to have been a member of the notorious Vasquez band."

Twain got into the death-on-the-frontier mix with his character Buck Fanshaw, a "representative citizen" of Virginia City and its philosopher king. Twain said that in the delirium of typhoid fever, Buck killed himself. On the inquest it was shown that he "had taken arsenic, shot himself through the body, cut his throat, and jumped out of a fourth-floor window and broken his neck." After deliberating the facts, the sad jury "with intelligence unblinded by its sorrow, brought in a verdict of death 'by the visitation of God.'" Twain marveled: "What would the world do without such juries?"[17]

Pleasure ladies were not immune to the endemic violence. A favorite lady of the night during Virginia City's heyday was Julia Bulette, a Louisiana damsel who had found her way to town from San Francisco, where she had apprenticed in her profession. In the beginning a sole practitioner, she eventually became the owner and madam of the largest and most prosperous brothel in the West.

Known for her good works, Juila was "the stereotypical whore with a heart of gold, she raised money for orphans, bought slaves out of bondage, took food and coffee to firemen, nursed sick and injured miners, and pressured city fathers to build cleaner cabins for her less fortunate sisters in their squalid shacks."[18] Her firemen friends (and clientele) awarded her an honorary membership in Virginia Engine Company Number One.

Alas, despite her good works, Julia did not receive the just dispensation of an all-wise Providence she had earned. In January 1867, at age thirty-five, she was murdered by a two-bit French drifter named Jean Millain, who, local insiders hypothesized, had been sent by Julia's resentful former San Francisco business associates. She was accorded a funeral in the finest Virginia City tradition,

---

[17] Twain, p. 172.
[18] Morris Jr., p. 111.

including a parade featuring the local militia band marching to a funeral dirge.

Julia's killer was tried and found guilty. He was hanged on April 24, 1868, still proclaiming his innocence. He had come to be known as "the man who martyred a madam."

It was pretty much agreed out on the frontier that "even if there is a God, he sure and hell ain't just." It was tough country and tough times. It's little wonder that the era would spawn men mean and daring enough to pull off the most spectacular train robbery and prison break in the history of the West; men who would leave innocents in their murderous wake.

4
Reno: Born of the Railroad

Before the silver strike at the Comstock and the advent of the railroad, commerce in the Truckee Meadows grew gradually due to the needs of immigrants headed for California. Crossing the Truckee River safely on a regular basis became a necessity. A ferryboat operation started in 1857 in the Glendale area east of modern downtown Reno. It was named Stone and Gates Crossing after its operators.

At about the same time, a man named John Stout built a toll bridge at a shallow spot on the Truckee five or so miles to the west nearer the Sierras. The bridge was purchased by John M. Hunter and renamed Hunter's Crossing.[19] Hunter operated a store and livery business known as Hunter's Station at the foot of the bridge near the mouth of a large side canyon. He thrived until his business foundered as a result of competition generated by the construction a few years later of the Central Pacific Railroad's depot in what would become Reno. Local landmarks still carry Hunter's name.

In 1859 rancher Charles F. Fuller of Susanville, California, eighty-five miles north of Reno, bought land on the south side of

---

[19] The train robbery described later in these pages took place near Hunter's Crossing.

the Truckee River adjacent to a long-used, shallow fording point. He built a toll bridge and called it Fuller's Crossing. Despite his prescience in seeing the need for a bridge and selecting the right location, Fuller was a poor businessman. It was said that before circumstances forced him to sell, he was down to wearing a blanket around his waist, having sold his trousers to pay for his whiskey.

In 1861 Fuller sold his holdings, including the toll bridge, to Myron Lake, a rancher from Honey Lake Valley between Reno and Susanville. The bridge became Lake's Crossing, and the surrounding area (today's downtown Reno) came to be known by that name. As his businesses prospered, Lake bought acreage on the north side of the Truckee to add to his holdings and constructed roads that converged on the bridge from several directions. He built a gristmill at the north end of the bridge and a luxurious hotel called the Lake House at the south end at a location that would eventually become the site of the Riverside Hotel. The facilities were on the principal road to booming Virginia City.

Today, the soon-to-be-replaced Virginia Street Bridge on Reno's main thoroughfare crosses the Truckee at the site of Fuller's and Lake's original crossing. "Lake's Crossing" has been preserved as the name of a state-owned facility for the diagnosis and treatment of mentally ill offenders located in Sparks, not far downstream from the bridge. Lake Street is a principal downtown Reno thoroughfare.

The route of the Central Pacific Railroad mapped by Theodore Judah would be east from Sacramento, through Dutch Flat, over the crest of the Sierras at Donner Pass, and down through the Truckee River Canyon to a station at Verdi and a depot in the Truckee Meadows. When he saw the maps, Lake realized the commercial possibilities. He offered a portion of his lands on the north side of the river to the railroad in return for a promise to put a station near his bridge. Leland Stanford agreed, and Lake became, along with the mining barons, one of Nevada's wealthiest men. In 1879 he purchased a mansion for his wife, but they were divorced two years later. The Lake Mansion, built by William Marsh in 1877, remains a Reno landmark.

Joseph Graham, a Central Pacific civil engineer, was in charge of constructing the railroad through Nevada. In April 1868, at a point about ten miles east of the base of the Sierras, he commenced a survey of the boundary of a thirty-five-acre parcel just north of the Truckee River and Lake's bridge. That parcel was eventually auctioned off in lots and would become downtown Reno.

Construction of the railroad over the Sierras was difficult and costly, as was anticipated early on by Congress. To illustrate, it took five years to construct 135 miles of track from Sacramento to Reno, but just one year to construct the remaining 490 miles of the Central Pacific's end of the line. The line reached Graham's town site in early 1868 on its way to hook up with the Union Pacific the next year in the Utah Territory at Promontory Summit north of the Great Salt Lake. On May 9, 1868, the city of Reno was officially born. The post office opened on May 13. As promised, Stanford directed that a depot be constructed on the land acquired from Myron Lake. In time Reno would supplant Virginia City as the population center of the then nearly four-year-old state of Nevada.[20]

The city was named after Major General Jesse Lee Reno, a decorated veteran of the Mexican-American War. He was killed in the Civil War during the Antietam Campaign by a Confederate sniper's bullet while commanding troops at Fox's Gap in the Battle of South Mountain on September 14, 1862. Several of his fellow officers, including General Irvin McDowell, the United States Army's Pacific commander, suggested that the new townsite be named after the late general. Charles Crocker agreed on behalf of the Central Pacific.

South Mountain, at the northern end of the Blue Ridge Mountains, is east of and visible from the Antietam battle site, where some twenty-three thousand Union and Confederate soldiers were killed or wounded on one hellacious day, September 17, 1862. Union forces were in pursuit of Robert E. Lee's Army of Northern Virginia, which had taken the offensive by moving north into Maryland. The pitched battles at Fox's Gap, where Reno died, and two nearby mountain passes were fought by Lee as delaying actions, leading to Antietam three days later.

---

[20] Nevada was granted statehood on October 31, 1864, just eight days before Lincoln's reelection. Its admission helped bolster antislavery sentiment in Congress. With its motto "Battle Born," the state's birth preceded the end of the Civil War by six months.

Whether the newly named town would prosper was a subject of remark by the railroad builders, one saying in effect (apologies to Gertrude Stein) that "there is no there there." As the railroad reached town, it was "at that point a small collection of squatters' shacks, tents, and many wooden stakes poking out of a light covering of snow."[21]

But things changed rapidly. Four months after the town was formed, a reporter for the *San Francisco Chronicle* foresaw its potential: "We arrived at Reno and here beheld another new town. The noise of hammer, and plane, and saw re-echoed on all sides, and the city rises like an exhalation. It is a complete mirage on the desert, and will probably be as magnificent."

It's been said that Reno was named after Marcus Reno, the commander of a US Army unit that survived George Armstrong Custer's infamous Battle of the Little Big Horn. However, the massacre of the troops at Little Big Horn, precipitated by Custer's poor judgment and rash bravado, occurred in June 1876, eight years after the city had been named in honor of General Jesse Lee Reno.

Although his reputation was tarnished to an extent as a result of government investigations of the Little Big Horn debacle, Marcus Reno had a meritorious military career. A graduate of West Point, he served as captain of a US Calvary regiment at Antietam. Six months later, on March 17, 1863, he was wounded in the Battle of Kelly's Ford, after which he was given the brevet rank of major for gallant conduct. Little more than three months after that, he fought as a cavalry officer in the battle at Gettysburg, the turning point in the Civil War.[22] Thus, Marcus Reno rather miraculously survived three of the most intense battles of that war, including two with the most casualties, as well as by far the most destructive battle—to the US Army if not the Indians—of the Indian campaign.

---

[21] Bain, p. 470.
[22] Custer played a significant role in the Union army's victory at Gettysburg.

The Fatal Affair in Monte Diablo Canyon

Reno, Nevada's namesake, Major General Jesse Lee Reno (1823 - 1862); U.S. Military Academy 1846

Major Marcus Reno (1834 - 1889); U.S. Military Academy 1857

CHAPTER 3

The First Train Robbery in the West

1
"The Whole Goddamn Payroll"

John Squiers had come to the Comstock to dig up his share of the riches, but it didn't take long for him to figure out that mining was dark and dangerous. His preference was stage robbery, which provided a far greater return for a fraction of the labor. He started his career in 1861 with a stage heist down the mountain from Virginia City in what newspapers called "the Flowery District in Six Mile Canon." He was assisted by men named Jack Davis and Tilton Cockerill, both of whom would join him again in a spectacular criminal venture a decade later. Squiers had wanted to visit his family in Connecticut, and the heist gave him "my raise to go east."

Nine years later on a coolish September evening, he's drinking heavily as he jaws and plays poker in Crittenden's elaborate gambling hall in Virginia City. They're talking about unsolved stage robberies. A bit more worldly and in his mind a lot smarter than his companions, Squiers throws out a Dickensian phrase he likes to bandy about: "The Law is a ass."[1] The boys roar and chip in for another round.

As Squiers acknowledges a beery toast, a man strides up to the table. "I ran into John Chapman yesterday in Reno. He says he has a big deal and wants you in. Wants to see you tomorrow at the Lake House. Four o'clock." Squiers tosses the man a nickel and points at the bar.

Squiers has had many a drink with John Chapman, a Canadian, a sometimes miner, and a regular Sunday school teacher whose colorful conversations mix profanities with quotes from the scriptures. He considers Chapman, despite his professed piety, to be as skilled in the dark arts as any man he's ever met.

The last time they talked during a poker game, Chapman complained about being ripped off by mine bosses and poker houses. The Lord had told him there was more in store for him, and he figured there were easier ways to get there than cards and shovels. "You know what I mean, John? I listen when the man upstairs talks," he had said.

---

[1] Spoken by Mr. Bumble in *Oliver Twist*.

So Squiers knows Chapman's "big deal" has nothing to do with poker or work. A weeks-long downer at the tables has him interested. But he's resolved: no more stage robberies; the law is too hot now.
Maybe Chapman has something new in mind.

As sunlight makes its way into his stuffy room in the boarding house on C Street the next morning, Squiers takes a hit from the nearly empty whiskey bottle sitting on the windowsill by his bed. It will ease his hangover and flavor his breath.

Sitting on the bed in ragged long johns, he takes a dishrag and sloshes cold water on his face from a tin basin on a chair and combs out his full, bushy beard. He gets up and looks at himself in a piece of cracked mirror hanging on the wall and grimaces to lift his lips as he cleans off his teeth. His finger slips across the space where a front tooth was knocked out in a barroom brawl. His bulbous nose shines back at him, and a permanent welt above his left eye tops off a visage roughened by hard times and bad choices.

He puts on his best pair of denim pants, tucks them into his miner's boots, and puts a black leather vest on over the freshly laundered shirt he'd hung on the doorknob in hope the wrinkles would smooth out. He tucks a single-shot derringer in one boot and an eight-inch knife in the other.

Outside someone says "hello, John," but Squiers, blinded as much by a throbbing headache as by the onerous morning sun, just snorts in reply. He passes churchgoers strolling along the board sidewalks, self-consciously resplendent in bowlers and frocks. He flips the stable-boy a nickel, saddles up, and heads down Geiger Grade toward the valley where he can get on the Carson-Reno road and head north.

Squiers is familiar with the cuts and angles and grades of the steep, switchback road, rutted from storm runoff and wagon traffic. Several times he and his confederates had robbed stagecoaches at night as they slowed to navigate the hairpin turns. On one occasion he'd paid off the shotgun messenger, letting him in on the action in return for his promise to keep his hands high and his gun in his lap. Another time the local judge was aboard, telling the sheriff he was relieved of his valuables by "a laughing masked man."

Lawmen had long suspected Squiers in a number of robberies, but they could never get the goods on him enough to convince Storey County's district attorney that he could get a conviction.

"Get me an eyewitness who can make a good identification, and we'll have our trial," was the prosecutor's ready reply. A good many of the citizenry thought he was either on the take or afraid.

James B. Hume, Wells Fargo's chief detective, had started assigning two shotgun messengers to each stage, along with outriders armed with Henry rifles to cover the flanks. The story on the streets and in the bars was that Hume had personally paid to have a warning etched on the tombstone of a road agent shotgunned by his men: "WELLS FARGO NEVER FORGETS."

Squiers hopes Chapman's big deal is something new because Hume has scared him straight out of the holdup business. He knows he can't make a living gambling, and he's sickened by the prospect of going into the mines and getting dirty to earn his keep.

Cutting the switchbacks as he prods his horse down the mountain, he wonders what Chapman is thinking. *Has he learned from the inside that a stage carrying payroll for one of the mines will be coming up the grade? Does he have plans to hit it?* Although Squiers had thought about holding up a payroll stage, he makes up his mind to tell Chapman that if that's the deal, he won't be part of it. He prefers being poor to the business end of a shotgun.

He gazes at Mount Rose capping the crest of the Carson Range across the valley, snowfields still covering the north-facing slopes along its upper flanks after a hard winter. The nights have been cold, and aspen groves abundant in the canyons show hints of autumn colors. He rounds a ridge and sees Peavine Mountain fifteen miles to the north past Reno, and below it the Truckee River Canyon where the new transcontinental railroad runs.

As he reaches Steamboat Valley at the bottom of the grade, he reins his horse off to the south and rides along a row of shimmering poplars planted by early settlers. The grass bends with the gentle breeze, mynahs swoop and bark, and chipmunks chatter among fallen dead trees. He takes off his vest and shirt, sloshes himself with warm water from a stream near Steamboat Hot Springs, and sits, soaking his feet, still wondering about Chapman. Idling, he cuts the tip off a fingernail and scratches the grime from under the rest of the nails with his knife. After finishing some hardtack, he bites off a plug.

Rested and restored, his hangover subsiding, he finds a cool stream and fills his canteen. He mounts up and sets out north on the last ten miles on the well-traveled road to Reno, his horse quickly working up a sweat in the afternoon heat. Dust begins to whip up in the ever-present wind as he avoids potholes and works his way through creeks and eroding ditches. He stops to talk and chew with a friend working on the new Virginia & Truckee Railroad line that will soon connect Carson City and Virginia City with transcontinental service in Reno.

Squiers leaves his horse at Lake's livery stable and walks across the street to the Lake House, making sure along the way that his coat covers the pistol stuck in his waistband. He scrapes the soles of his boots on the hotel steps and dusts off his clothes. He worries that guests will catch his scent even though he'd cleaned up along the way.

He finds John Chapman in the saloon. He feels out of place in Reno's most ornate surroundings, especially as he moves to sit by the slick-dressing, smooth-talking Chapman.

The slender Chapman's black pants and waistcoat are clean and pressed, his V-shaped beard neatly trimmed. He's smoking a long, brown hand-rolled cigarette. Black bowler, cigarette papers, and a small cloth bag of Turkish tobacco sit on the bar next to his gin and tonic. He turns and reaches out a hand with a wave and smile.

Squiers coughs out a guttural greeting and nods as he pulls up a stool and throws down the double whiskey Chapman had ordered. He takes a deep breath and begins to relax. He looks in the gilt-edged mirror behind the bar and takes off his slouchy miner's hat and smoothes his hair.

"What's up, Chapman? What's the big deal you wanted to see me about?"

After small talk, Chapman gets to the point. "Thanks for coming down. I need to talk to someone I can trust about something that's been on my mind. Something big for these parts." He taps his glass with a coin and signals for another drink.

"You know, while I'm sitting around here, I hear a lot of talk." He pauses until the bartender is out of earshot. "Most don't amount to anything, but sometimes the railroad men drink too much at the poker table. When they're drunk, they talk, and I listen and sometimes join in. They talk a lot about train robberies back east, especially the first one in Indiana. One of them knew the fireman and he never quits talking about how it was pulled off."

"Yeah, everybody's heard about that." Squiers holds up a hand to interrupt Chapman and signals the barkeep for another whiskey. "Bring it with a water back." He turns back to Chapman and cups his ear like he wants to hear more.

Chapman looks down, fingers circling his glass. He speaks softly without looking at Squiers. "Listen, John, I got thinking and looking around and asking questions. What I found is there's more money coming to town on the railroad every week than's on a year's worth of those stage cars going up to Virginia. The payroll for some of the mines up there comes right on down the tracks from Frisco."

After a pause for a reply, Chapman straightens up and looks Squiers squarely in the eyes. Quietly but forcefully, he says, "Jesus, John, listen to me. The whole … goddamn … payroll!"

Squiers smiles wryly as Chapman curses. He's often heard Chapman tell how he teaches the kids in his Sunday Bible school class not to use the Lord's name in vain or the devil will be on the doorstep. But Squiers knows the game. Like a lot of the pious folk on the frontier, Chapman appeases the Lord by using Sunday to cleanse his soul after dirtying it the rest of the week.

"Lord knows it's there for the taking. I've heard a lot and read about a lot about them trains being knocked off all the time back east, but it hasn't happened out this way." Chapman flashes Squiers a grin, looking like he's hit a straight flush. "At least not yet."

Squiers tilts his stool back and looks up at the ceiling, hands behind his head, thinking.

"You know," Chapman goes on, "they just aren't ready for something like that out here. There's a lot more open space and a lot fewer law men, and none of them are on the trains. It'd be easy. Board the train when it slows and surprise the trainmen with shotguns. They'd have no chance, and there'd be no help anywhere near."

He sips his drink while looking directly at Squiers. "They don't have Well Fargo agents on these express trains, either," he says, as if anticipating a question.

Squiers doesn't reply. He doesn't altogether fathom what he's heard, but he knows that a payroll for the Virginia City mines, just one of them, is a hell of a lot of gold.

Chapman flips his cigarette butt at a spittoon. It misses, and he ups and grinds it on the floor with his heel. Leaning an elbow on the bar, he nods at the bartender and points at his glass. He turns to expertly rolling smokes that he carefully places in his tobacco bag.

After a few minutes Squiers rises and jerks his head toward the door. "Let's go out by the river and talk."

They're back in the bar, feeling the effects of drink.

"We meet here again in two weeks. You'll hear from me," Chapman says. He raises his glass to toast Squiers, and they tap glasses.

"What are the odds, Chapman? I mean, it seems like a good idea but it'll be dangerous. They might not have agents on the train, but you can bet Wells Fargo detectives will be out full bore. If they nail us, we'll spend a lot of time locked up in Carson."

"I haven't heard of anyone getting caught hitting trains, and they've scored a lot of gold."

Squiers pauses and looks quizzically at Chapman. He strokes his beard with one hand as he fingers his glass with the other. "Sounds like good odds, but, you know, it'll take more than the two of us to pull off something like that."

"You bet. We sure enough need more men, but let me work up the plan first. Meantime, we both think about who we can trust to bring in."

"I've got someone in mind already," Squiers says. "You know Jack Davis."

"I thought about him myself," Chapman says. "But let's wait a bit. I'll first get down to Frisco and see if I can figure out which train we hit and where we do it. Then when we get Davis and some others in, we can meet at the joint Chat Roberts has in Long Valley."

"Nobody will care about some gamblers and dirty miners hanging out and drinking way the hell up there."

"Chat'll keep his mouth shut."

After a few more drinks, Chapman rises. "I'm going over to the station and get the train schedule." He reaches to shake hands with Squiers's. "We're on to something, John."

"Yeah, Chapman, we sure'n hell are." Squiers gets off the bar stool. "We sure'n hell are," he says, laughing as he slaps Chapman on the back.

November 1870 timetable for the Central Pacific Railroad.

Central Pacific station, Reno, c. 1872. (Courtesy of Nevada Historical Society)

The Lake House Hotel, Reno. (Courtesy of Nevada Historical Society)

2
"God Almighty, Can You Believe It's Sixty Thousand?"

The next day Chapman buys a ticket on the Central Pacific train west. He pores over the schedule of trains coming back to Reno from San Francisco, napping sporadically during the daylong trip over the Sierras to Sacramento. He boards another train and debarks at the Long Wharf in Oakland and takes the ferry to San Francisco, where he takes a room at the Coso House on Sansome Street.

Usually dressed like a prosperous gambler, he has an amiable personality that masks his continual search for an easy mark; he makes friends easily. After buying a few rounds he learns from a drunken railroad account clerk in the hotel saloon that the payroll for the Yellow Jacket Mine, Gold Hill's richest property, will be on the Central Pacific's *Overland Express* leaving San Francisco on November 4, 1870. On its runs to Ogden, Utah, the *Overland* leaves Oakland eastbound at 8:30 a.m. and is scheduled through Reno seventeen hours later at 1:15 a.m.

Damn, it's perfect. Square in the middle of the night.

He decides the place to stop the train is east of the Verdi station where, after crossing the mountains, the tracks flatten out and head into the vastness of Nevada. It's unlikely anyone will be around when the *Overland* reaches the station after midnight. His men can board the train after it stops to drop the mail and begins to get back up to speed.

Back in Reno, he looks up Sol Jones, a longtime friend he knows he can trust who can act as a liaison with Squiers. Jones is at his favorite rail-workers' bar in the seedy commercial area along the tracks east of Lake Street. They move off to a corner of the wood-frame and canvas structure, and Chapman orders drinks.

Chapman says, "Let me tell you about an idea of mine. I think you might be interested." He details Jones as to what he and Squiers have cooked up.

Jones doesn't hesitate. "Hit a train? God damn! No one around here would ever suspect something like that. Hell yes, I'm in, Chapman," he says with a grin.

With a finger to his lips, Chapman signals Jones to keep his voice down. "It's a good deal. The odds are good to make a big stake."

"I could sure'n hell use a stake right now, I tell you. The mines ain't hiring, and I've been on a bad run." Skinny and pale, Jones has a frazzled look, fading blond hair mussed, dirty clothes a size to large. His appearance befits the size of his bank roll.

Chapman says, "Squiers is going to talk to Jack Davis about coming in. Meantime, you and me can do some looking around and plan this thing out some more."

"I know Squiers pretty well. I can work with him. Don't know Davis."

"He's one of them that did the stage job with Squiers in Six Mile a few years back down by Gold Hill."

"I heard about that job."

Chapman and Jones saddle up and ride west toward Verdi, scouting along the tracks for a place to stop the train. They find a culvert by the tracks near a switch not far from Hunter's Station, a little more than halfway to Verdi, six miles or so west of Reno.

"This is where we block the tracks," Chapman says. "You'll be posted here."

Squiers shows up at the Lake House with his stage-robbing crony Jack Davis, who had worked a few jobs with Chapman. Chapman reaches out his hand to Davis. They get a table in the back of the bar where they won't be overheard. Jones enters and joins in as they roll dice for drinks and smokes.

Chapman explains the plan he and Squiers have concocted.

"Hit a train! That's what Squiers was telling me." Davis tilts his chair backward, chortling as he taps a finger on his temple beneath his wide black Stetson. "Hell of an idea. Goddamn law around here won't suspect nothin'."

He realizes he's loud and lets his chair drop back. He nods at Squiers, talking quietly. "Me and John here," he says as he pats Squiers on the arm, "we're laying off the stages. Wells Fargo's got shotgun riders every damn way a man looks. A payroll train will work just fine for me, Chapman." He takes a slender cheroot from inside his heavy long black coat and scratches a match on the table. He sits back, smoking, stroking his beard and nodding as he listens.

"Chapman went to Frisco and cased the operation. The payroll will be for the Yellow Jacket," Squiers says.

"I never liked the bastards who run that mine. Gyp a man out of pay any way they can." Davis pauses and looks at Chapman. "It ain't going to be hard to take their money."

"Damn sure," Squiers says.

After a few rolls of the dice for more drinks, Chapman lays out the plan. "It'll be the *Overland Express*. It leaves Frisco early morning on the fourth of November and is due in Reno after midnight. Wells Fargo will be here in Reno to meet the train and pick up the payroll and stage it on up to Virginia."

"We stop the train out toward Verdi," Jones says. "The payroll will never reach the stage."

Chapman says, "I'll go down to Frisco again and make sure the payroll is on the train that day. I'll send a coded wire to Jones if there's enough gold on board to be worth the risk. It'll be dead of night when you do the job."

He nods at Davis. "You're right. Just like you said, it'll be a total surprise to the train crew."

Chapman takes a pencil and napkin and draws a map showing the railroad snaking along the Truckee between Reno and Verdi. "You men board at Verdi and separate the express car and engine from the rest of the train as you go down the line. That's how they pulled it off back east. Then you stop the engine here, close to Hunter's Station, where me an Jones marked a spot."

"Force the crew to open the express car where the coin will be bagged. There might be a locked treasure box too. Split up some of the take, bury the rest, and scatter until the heat is off. It could be months."

Squiers says, "Me and Davis will find a place to get ready for the hit. Somewhere up in the Peavine foothills, close above the tracks and Hunter's place."

"Every man brings his horse and gun," Davis says. "I'll bring me a shotgun. Ain't never shot a man, but I ain't robbed a railroad either, and I damn sure ain't going to do ten to twenty for it."

"Okay," Chapman says. "Meantime, we need to line up some more men. Since I'll be in Frisco and Jones will be down by the tracks, we'll need more men than just you two to board the train."

"I know another man I can line up quick," Squiers says. "Tilton Cockerill. He was with us when me and Davis did the stage job in Six Mile in '61. He's living up in Virginia and working the mines, the poor bastard. He's a hell of a horseman, so I don't know why he's doing that kind of work."

"I know him. Bring him in," Chapman says.

Chapman rolls a cigarette and takes a long drag. "That makes five so far," he says as he exhales, "but the way I have it figured, we still need more men."

"Shit, Chapman, more men just means more ways to screw up and smaller shares." Davis slaps his knee.

"I disagree, Jack. More men means more eyes, more ears, more guns."

Chapman waits for Squiers or Davis to argue. "Let's get on up to Virginia," he finally says. "I know some other men might want to join us."

They spot Jim Gilchrist the next afternoon in the Sawdust Corner Saloon. He's a Virginia City miner who's been in poker games with Squiers and Chapman and heard them talking about stage heists.

Chapman says, "I'll talk to Gilchrist. Good man. Not much of a talker, and he keeps what he's heard to himself."

Chapman pulls up a stool, rolls cigarettes, and offers one to Gilchrist. After they swap stories and Chapman buys Gilchrist enough whiskey to loosen him up, Chapman says, "Come on outside where we can talk. I got a deal might interest you."

Walking along the wooden sidewalk, they pass gamblers and ladies of the night on evening parade, and dust-covered miners fresh up from the shafts. The bars are alive and loud.

"You know, Jim, me and Squiers been thinking about lightening up a train of some payroll money." Chapman says it like it's hypothetical, but he gets specific when Gilchrist cocks his head to listen. "We got all the details pretty much down. It's never been done around here, and it'll be a snap. Easy take if you want in."

Gilchrist looks at Chapman with raised eyebrows. "You really intend to rob the railroad?"

Chapman says, "Yep. We figure we can pull it off when the law won't have a chance of catching us. We'll be splitting up more gold than we could mine in a hundred years."

Like Sol Jones, Gilchrist is a naive sort and near broke. He's a native of Ireland, born in County Down. His bright red hair and heavy accent make it seem like he just left the old country. He reached California as the gold rush days were waning and rode back east over the Sierras in 1863, looking for better prospects. He makes just enough working the mines for room and board and to pay his tabs in the saloons.

Gilchrist's Irishness has made his life hard. Many of the townspeople equate Irish laborers with blacks, both of them a rung or two down the social ladder from the Chinese, who own most of Virginia's laundries and restaurants.

A favorite character immortalized by Mark Twain in *Roughing It* was Buck Fanshaw, Virginia City's best-known citizen. He was the proprietor of the busiest saloon, a canny politician, and a barroom philosopher who was esteemed by the citizenry. The sign above the ornate bar in his saloon barked out prejudices that were not uncommon: "NO IRISH NEED APPLY."

"The railroad. Damn. Let me think a minute, Chapman," Gilchrist says. "Let's go back in and you can give me some more details. I'll buy us a couple."

After more drink and small talk, Gilchrist rationalizes his decision. "I ain't never taken nothing wasn't mine without having confessed to the priest. But the mine people are taking my life, so's you can count me in. If they can take a man's work without paying him a fair wage, why sure as the devil is in hell a man can take some o' their money."

They sit quietly while Gilchrist sips his whiskey. "There ain't no priest on this side of the mountains. Seein' one o' them was the only thing made me feel guilty enough to find a confession booth anyway. I got nothing to lose, Chapman."

Chapman slaps him on the back. "Jim, you're about to make a big stake."

Squiers finds E. B. Parsons in the stable down the street about to mount and ride down to Gold Hill. With occasional stints in the mines to tide him over after big losses, Parsons has made a living as a professional gambler. Born in New Hampshire, he'd headed west after serving on the Union side in the war and finding there were no jobs back home. He still sports the bushy mustache he grew as a soldier. He dresses flashier than miners and prefers pointed-toe gambler's boots, all to create the illusion of success at the tables.

Squiers says, "Parsons, come and have a drink with me and Jack Davis."

"I ain't in no rush. What's up?"

"C'mon, we'll talk."

In a dark corner of the Bucket of Blood, whiskey bottle on the table, Squiers says, "I know you ain't never been no squealer. So let me tell you what me and Davis and the boys have in mind. We're gonna get ourselves a quick raise."

Parsons hears Squiers out. "Jesus, that's some plan. Who's 'the boys' you're talking about?"

"Me and Jack here, and John Chapman, Sol Jones, and maybe a couple more."

"Sounds like a gamble with better odds than I usually get." Parsons smiles and raises his glass in a toast. "Hell, yes. Count me in on that one. I like your thinking."

"We'll be meeting to do some planning at Chat Roberts's place in Long Valley," Davis says. "You'll hear from me or Squiers."

Back at the Sawdust Corner, Chapman is finally satisfied with the manpower. He writes down the names of the men on the back of his map and jabs Squiers on the shoulder. "I haven't seen ol' Cockerill yet, let's find him and I'll buy us all a drink."

They locate Cockerill jawing with a miner on the stoop of the office of the *Territorial Enterprise*. He's a good sized man, a skilled horseman, strong and in shape, with a steely gray eyes and long auburn hair. He's had a few two many run-ins with the law and hates the Wells Fargo agents who spy around town. They trust him. The three men wander off to Crittenden's where it's less crowded.

A drunk Squiers says, "Chapman, this is it. No more goddamn mines, and no more chasing stages."

"All I need is enough take to get me back to Illinois," Cockerill says. "Don't take much to live out on the edge near the river where I came from."

"The fourth of November is coming up quick. When we get that gold, I'm going to pack up and get down to Frisco and do some living," Chapman says.

"Shit, I ain't thought about how to spend it," Squiers says. "But it won't take me long."

The men touch shot glasses, throw down the drinks, and signal for another order.

The whole group meets for the first time at Chat Roberts's saloon in Long Valley, twenty miles up the Susanville Road from Reno. It's a sunny October afternoon, and they're sitting by the creek in an aspen grove where Roberts has placed chairs around a table fashioned out of a broken wagon wheel.

An apron-clad Roberts brings out a tray of beers and Chapman flips him a coin. Although he has heard their boozy talk, Roberts is not in on the deal.

Chapman pulls out his map and starts through the plan. "It'll be the fourth of November; actually the early morning of the fifth when you stop the train. But everything is off unless I wire the okay to Jones. Like I been saying, four men get on board here at Verdi," he says, pointing. "They stop the train here by Hunter's where we'll have the tracks blocked."

He nods at Squiers. "John will take the lead boarding the train and get up to the engineer and take the lead. He'll keep in touch with you over the next couple of weeks and fill in the details. He'll communicate with me through Sol when I'm in Frisco."

Squiers spits a wad of chew over his shoulder into the creek. "We need lanterns and some grub while we wait for the train. Maybe some blankets. I found a shaft on Peavine where we can store the stuff."

"When do you want the rest of us up there?" Gilchrist says.

"All of us except Jones and Chapman get there on the third, Thursday, the day before the train heads this way."

A week before the scheduled date, the cabal meets again at the Roberts place. They light a fire in a pit along the creek, out of earshot. Some sit on tree stumps while the others stand. Davis throws a knife repeatedly at a heart someone had carved on an aspen.

J. B. Roberts, the son of Chat Roberts, brings out a bottle of whiskey and tin cups. After he leaves Chapman says, "I'm off for Frisco tomorrow."

He looks at Jones. "I'll wire you on the fourth around noon saying go or no go. Pick the wire up at the Western Union in Reno. When you read it, you'll know what it means. Either way, get quick up to Peavine and let these men know."

Squiers speaks up. "The shaft where we hole up is in the rolling hills directly across from Hunter's Canyon. You can see the railroad tracks down below."

He holds a whiskey as he draws in the dirt with a stick. "This is the track and road, and that there will be the shaft where we meet up," he says, pointing. "You can't miss it. A steep wash leads straight to it, and I'll mark the cutoff point by rocks piled on the side of the road. You men except Jones be there by noon on Thursday. I'll be watching from above and guide anybody who can't figure how to get up there."

"I'll be on the train back to Reno from Frisco a day or so after the job's done, Chapman says. "Take a few coins to tide you over until we split the take, every man an equal share. Davis will bury most of it until its safe."

Davis says, "Me and Chapman will let you know when we divide it out."

They leave it at that and pass the whiskey bottle around. Chapman drinks gin from his hip flask. They don't bother fashioning alibis should any of them be nabbed by the law. They chew and spit and get drunk until night begins to fall. The die is cast.

After a long lull, Chapman says, "How about a little prayer, boys? Won't hurt to ask the Lord to light the way."

Squiers gets up to walk to his horse. "We don't need your 'Lord,' Chapman. He ain't never helped anyone I know." Turning around, he spits out his plug and points at the group. His eyes are dark like his beard and menacingly ardent. "Anyone who rats won't be walking the earth very long."

Davis kicks a half-burned log sticking out of the fire and sparks fly into the darkening sky. "You got that right, Squiers," he says with pursed lips as he hitches his pants. "You and me will make that a goddamn sure thing." He motions for Cockerill to follow, and the three men mount and head into the darkness.

As Chapman leaves to speak with Chat Roberts, Jones motions with his head for Gilchrist to follow him into the saloon. The sawdust Roberts tries to keep fresh on the floor is piled mostly against the bar under the foot rail. The spittoons haven't been emptied, and the place smells like tobacco and stale beer. They stand at a corner of the bar where the light from the ceiling lantern is dim, obscured by the smoke from damp wood burning in a fireplace in the corner.

Jones says with a low voice, "Jim, you been pretty quiet acting, like maybe you ain't too happy being in this. Myself, I wonder. You think we can pull this off?"

Gilchrist shrugs. "It sounds almost too easy to me. How about you? You think something's wrong?" he says in his deep Irish brogue.

"Yeah. I got me a gut feeling, but we can't pull out now. What the hell, I guess it's a go. The only way it ain't is if I get the wire from Chapman saying it's not on."

Gilchrist takes a long swig from his mug and pauses before he talks, looking down, thinking. "If the payroll ain't on this train," he finally says, "then that's it for me. I ain't in on nothing else."

Jones shrugs and shakes his head. He says without looking up, "Truth be told, I ain't never been on edge like I am now. I wish I wasn't in."

"Yeah, I know. Believe me, I know."

Sol Jones lingers in a saloon on the bank of the Truckee, nervously sipping cold coffee and backing it with shots. Looking at the train schedule, he figures the *Overland Express* is somewhere near Auburn on the California side, starting the long, slow climb over the Sierras. It's afternoon, and the wind chills him as he ups and crosses the dusty street to the Western Union office. Davis had told him the wire from Chapman would be signed "Joseph Enrique."

Where the hell did they come up with that name?

"Telegram for Sol Jones?" he asks through the bars of the clerk's cage.

The clerk glances up, his eyes shaded by a visor. He sifts through a stack of messages, pushes a receipt under the cashier window for Jones to sign, and slides a telegram under the bars.

Jones doesn't want to read it. He folds and puts it in his vest pocket. He buttons his coat and heads for the stable by the depot, his reluctance to face the events he's begun to fear reflected in his lumbering walk. He mounts and rides to the Hills Stable where he picks up Cockerill's newly shoed horse, Cock-a-doodle. With the second horse in tow, he rides up Virginia Street and turns west on Fourth Street toward Verdi. After a mile, he stops under an oak tree and opens the telegram. He holds it near his body to shield it from light snowflakes blowing haphazardly in the wind.

"SEND ME SIXTY DOLLARS TONIGHT WITHOUT FAIL. STOP. J. ENRIQUE."

He slumps in the saddle, eyes closed. *God, what am I doing?* After a minute, he straightens up and takes a deep breath. *Oh, what the hell.* Gathering himself, he sets a rapid gait for Peavine Mountain.

Then the realization sets in. "It means sixty thousand dollars! Goddamn," he says out loud. His day brightens. "Yes!"

Dust swirls in the distance along the road, the old immigrant trail that parallels the Central Pacific tracks along the Truckee. He's glad no riders are headed his way. Halfway to Verdi, he turns north and follows the ravine Squiers has marked. He welcomes the shadows of the lengthening afternoon as he rides slowly to keep the dust down.

He sees Squiers fifty yards above, squatting on a bare, reddish, rocky bluff, a shotgun across his lap. Squiers spots him and stands.

"Squiers, it's me, Sol Jones."

Squiers waves and clambers down through boulders and disappears.

"It's a go, it's a go," Jones excitedly says to the men coming out of the mine shaft as he dismounts. "Sixty thousand," he says, holding up five fingers and a one. "God almighty. Can you believe it's sixty thousand?"

He flashes a grin and walks over and pisses on a rock near the tunnel entrance. Shaking his head he mutters, "Sixty thousand. My God."

As Cockerill uncaps a whiskey bottle, Squiers yells at him. "Hey, this ain't no time for that! We got a job to do tonight. Chrissakes."

"Yes, goddamn it," Davis says. "Ain't no sixty thousand here yet. It's still coming up from Frisco. Couple of weeks when we're flush and things die down we can find us some women and drink all night."

"Sorry," Cockerill says, "but I'm dry, and I ain't going to do the job dry." He takes a long slug from the bottle and runs a sleeve across his mouth. He grins as he sighs in mock contentment.

"Shit, Cockerill," Davis says, shaking his head.

They move into the tunnel and have a bacon and coffee supper and pass around hardtack. Davis cuts slices off a plug and passes them around. As day turns to dusk, they ride single file down through the ravine.

Jones leads them to the switch alongside the tracks that he and Chapman had marked. Davis shinnies a pole and cuts the telegraph wires. The others stack a pile of railroad ties alongside the tracks.

"I'll block the tracks right after the freight train comes through," Jones says. "Should be an hour before the *Overland*."

"Put the lantern square in the middle of the tracks where we can see it," Squiers says.

After the others leave, the rigors of the day steal over Jones. He makes his way down to the Truckee River where he stretches out on grassy bank still holding the sun's warmth and dozes off to the murmur of swirling waters.

Squiers, Parsons, and Cockerill ride west toward the Sierras on the immigrant road in the fading light. Gilchrist and Davis follow higher up on a trail along the foothills. Lanterns at ranches across the river and at the homes of railroad workers around Verdi begin to flicker in the distance.

They assemble in a ravine at a bend in the Truckee a half mile east of the station at Verdi and sit on rocks in the dark to wait out the last hours. The snorts of restless horses are all that break the silence as they pass around Cockerill's courage-filled whiskey bottle. They watch in silence as the freight train coming down the tracks ahead of the *Overland* snakes by.

As the night blackens, Gilchrist leans against a rock in the star shadow and notices how the lights at Verdi and the burning tips of the men's smokes blend in with the stars lying low over the ridges. The plan they've concocted sits jagged and edgewise in his brain; it seems like even the silence is nervous.

The freight's whistle awakens Jones as midnight nears. He crouches below the riverbank until the train passes and then piles ties across the track. The *Overland* will be next; its whistle as it nears Verdi will give him warning. He lights a lantern and shrouds it with a red bandana.

"Let's ride!" Davis shouts as the *Overland*'s whistle sounds up the canyon.

A hundred yards short of the Verdi station, Squiers, Davis, Parsons, and Gilchrist dismount and walk toward the station's gas lamp. Cockerill leaves to lead the horses back to where they left Jones.

With a screech, the *Overland* downs brakes and pulls slowly into the station. A clerk leaps out of the express car and tosses a mailbag into the telegraph room. As the train coasts away toward Reno, the men, bandanas across their faces, run alongside and pull themselves aboard.

Davis and Squiers get on the back of the locomotive and scramble forward to the cab. They pull six-shooters on the engineer and fireman.

"You're dead men if you try a damn thing!" Squiers yells at the top of his voice.

The shocked engineer, Hank Small, raises his hands.

"Get your goddamn hands back where you can run this thing!"

Small lowers his hands and turns toward the control panel. The fireman stumbles backward and sits against the cab wall, arms around his knees, head bowed. Davis squats and trains a pistol on him.

Gilchrist posts himself on the front of the express car; Parsons is at the rear. The conductor sees Parsons and rushes out of the passenger car. "Get off this train. Get off!" When he lifts his lantern to get a better look he sees a revolver pointed at his face. The man holding it is masked.

"Tell me your name, conductor. Tell me the name of the express car man too."

"I'm Marshall. His name is Minchell."

"Okay, now get back there in that car and sit down, Marshall, and make it quick, or this gun might just go off."

The conductor retreats into the passenger car and closes the door. Parsons and Gilchrist wait for the signal for them to act.

Squiers presses his pistol against the engineer's temple. "Down the brakes exactly when I tell you."

The frightened Small misunderstands and blows the whistle to signal the brakemen to down the brakes. Squiers thumps him hard on the shoulder with the butt of his pistol and yells, "Do that again before I give the order, and I'll blow your goddamn head off!"

A mile down track from Verdi, Squiers pokes Small. "Blow the whistle twice, real quick and short."

For Parsons and Gilchrist on the express car, the double whistle is the signal to cut the bell cord and pull the coupling pin at the rear of the car. The locomotive and the mail and express cars separate from the rest of the train.

"Giver her steam, full bore," Davis yells from where he sits. He turns to the fireman and points at the boiler. "More wood."

Squiers jabs Small again. The shortened train starts its four mile run to where Jones has the tracks blocked. The engineer mumbles inaudibly; his clenched jaw shows defiance, but he obeys at gunpoint.

Squiers spots the red glow of the lantern on the track. "Power down, Small, and stop this side of the lantern."

As the cars come to a stop, Parsons leaps to the ground and bangs on the door of the express car.

"Who's there?"

"It's Marshall," Parsons yells. "Open the door, Minchell. We got a problem."

Parson's double-barrel shotgun is in Minchell's face as the express man slides the door open. "Good Lord," Minchell says as he reflexively throws up an arm. He will tell investigators later it was like staring into barrels as big as stovepipes.

"Shut up, and back off, and sit over there," Parsons says, gesturing toward a corner of the car as he gets into it.

Davis orders the engineer and fireman out of the locomotive. "Where's the shotgun, Jones? Where's the shotgun?" Jones rushes up with a shotgun.

Gun in one hand, Davis grabs an axe in the other and climbs into the express car. Parsons and Davis throw out bags of gold coin. In their hurry, they miss $8,000 in silver bars and ignore envelopes holding thousands of dollars worth of negotiable commercial paper.

"Thanks for not putting up a fight, Minchell. I didn't want to kill you." Parsons wags his gun at Minchell and laughs as he jumps out of the car.

It's over fast, quicker even than they had planned.

"Ride like hell," Davis yells. He takes the bulk of the take and rides into the darkness.

Jones and Cockerill put coins in a barley sack and ride east, staying well above the river road. They stop to water their horses at a spring near Red Rock where Cockerill buries the coins. Jones heads north as Cockerill turns toward Reno, leading horses left by Squiers, Parsons, and Gilchrist.

The latter three men had previously discussed the details of a getaway. Figuring it would be a good way to get the law off track, they decided to back-track in the direction the train had come from, toward the mountains. Tracks of horses would be easy to follow, so they would walk back to Verdi and cross the Sierra foothills into sparsely populated country across the California line where Squiers had once lived.

The three head west, walking quickly, stepping on ties to avoid leaving footprints, occasionally walking the rails. They move off into the darkness when they spot the rest of the train coasting down the track.

After the front cars were separated, Marshall, the conductor, had allowed the remaining cars of the engineless train to coast down the grade toward Reno. He signals the brakeman to set brakes when he sees the locomotive and express car. Hank Small and the fireman are removing blockage from the tracks.

"Thought sure I'd find you dead," Marshall says.

"We're lucky you didn't," Small replies. "Make no bones about it. That guy would have shot me if I tried anything. Heard the other guy call him 'Squeers' or something like that."

The train is made up again and reaches Reno just thirty minutes behind schedule. The severed telegraph lines prevent messages from going back to Central Pacific headquarters in Sacramento.

The Wells Fargo agent at Virginia City finally gets the word from Minchell just after sun-up. The agent wires Washoe County sheriff Charley Pegg at Washoe City: "Train robbed between Truckee and Verdi; robbers gone south." He has the location off by ten miles or more, but the hunt is on.

3
"It Almost Took the Public Breath Away"

*W*hen word of the robbery hit the wires, it caused such excitement that it came to be referred to as "the Great Robbery" in newspapers in the United States and Europe. One writer sought to capture the enormity of the event.

> This being the first train robbery in the world, it almost took away the public breath and for a while caused great excitement and much newspaper comment on two continents.
>
> Every enemy of law and order was vociferous in the praise of the boldness and nerve of the perpetrators, and Nevada acquired the dubious credit of being the first in the Union that could produce a set of outlaws daring enough to stop and rob an express train.[1]

Alas, it wasn't the first train robbery in the country, let alone the world; four years earlier, Indiana had earned that dubious credit, thanks to the Reno and Sparks boys. The heist between Verdi and Reno was, however, the first train robbery in the Far West and the first of the transcontinental railroad.

Washoe County, the state of Nevada, the Central Pacific Railroad, and the Wells Fargo Express Company posted rewards aggregating $30,000, which was thought to be the amount stolen. An audit soon showed, however, that the robbers had gotten away with over $41,000 in gold coin.

Washoe County undersheriff James H. Kinkead was put in charge of the effort to catch the robbers. Like Inspector Javert, the pursuer of thief-turned-solid-citizen Jean Valjean in Victor Hugo's *Les Misérables*, he would be relentless.

Kinkead and Sheriff Pegg saddled up in Washoe City south of Reno and struck for Hunter's Crossing. They took a shortcut along

---

[1] See Kinkead, p. 1. His report was edited later to make clear this was one of the early US train robberies, but not the first.

a road that ran between Truckee and Virginia City. It was a logical escape route should the robbers circle Reno and head for the relative safety of the Nevada outback off to the southeast. But it had snowed lightly, and it became apparent that no one had been on the road. They returned to Washoe City in time for Kinkead to take the 9:00 p.m. Dwyer stage to Reno.

The next morning Kinkead rode west along the railroad tracks to the spot where the robbers had stopped the train. He found a footprint distinguishable from others in the area. Writing about it years later, he described it as being "made by a boot having a very small heel, such as the dudes and gamblers wore in those days and our wives and daughters wear now."

No boot prints headed east toward Reno. As Kinkead rode the other direction along the tracks, he began to spot the prints intermittently. He realized the man had been walking on the ties and the rail to avoid leaving prints, and two men in miner's boots were with him. Four miles back near the train station at Verdi, the prints left the railroad and headed north through crusted snow up Dog Valley Creek, over Dog Valley Hill, and into Sardine Valley just inside California.

At the Sardine Valley House, the only place in the area that offered room and board, he identified himself as a law officer. The proprietress told him she knew of the train robbery. Three men had shown up just about daylight a day before and asked for rooms and supper, paying her with gold coins. She thought it odd they were without horses. Two of the men left early the next morning, but one was still in his room when Jim Burke and a group of deer hunters from Truckee arrived for breakfast.[2] They were eating when a fellow from Truckee stopped by with news of the robbery.

As they sat listening to the details, she looked out the window and saw the man she thought was still in his room. He was headed toward the privy, limping and looking around like he was being followed. She pointed him out to the hunters; they rushed out, questioned him at gunpoint, and put him under citizens' arrest. After

---

[2] James Burke, from Steamboat Springs, south of Reno, was a mining partner of James Marshall. Marshall's discovery of gold at Sutter's Mill on the American River in 1848 was the catalyst for the California gold rush.

telling her he was one of the train robbers, they left to turn him over to the sheriff in Truckee.

As to the two men who left before the deer hunters arrived, she told Kinkead one wore fancy boots that looked like they weren't much for walking. She described him as being well dressed considering that he was on foot. He said he was going to Loyalton. The other wore a bushy beard, was raggedy looking, and had a mean stare. He didn't talk and kept off to himself.

This was enough for Kinkead to hazard a guess that the bushy-bearded man was John Squiers from Virginia City. Kinkead knew Squiers had a brother, Joe, in nearby Sierraville, which confirmed his suspicion that he had the right man.

It was ten o'clock at night, but Kinkead was determined to press on, first to Loyalton. He had been there before on the road in from the east, but it was due north now. As she served him a of bowl stew, the proprietress told him that he could get lost and end up off to the west in Downieville or the Webber Lake vicinity.

She left and returned with a boy Kinkead figured to be about fourteen. Kinkead paid him ten dollars to lead the way, but with the understanding that, in case the robbers were encountered, the boy would turn back and let Kinkead fight it out alone. After an eight-mile ride through wind and snow, they reached Loyalton about midnight.

Kinkead located the only hotel in Loyalton. He entered quietly and startled the proprietor, who was snoozing in a chair by a flickering candle. Kinkead showed his badge and asked if anyone had arrived on foot. The proprietor said a man had come in a few hours earlier and staggered to his room without taking dinner.

The proprietor carried a lantern to the corridor and pointed to Room 4. Kinkead inched toward the room, the proprietor behind him with lantern in outstretched arm. Kinkead kept his rifle pointed ahead, finger on the trigger. Since the new hotel had not been painted, damp weather had caused the doors of the rooms to swell to the point that the door to Room 4 could not be closed nearly tight enough to lock. A chair had been placed under the inside doorknob. Kinkead was able to remove it and edge into the room without disturbing the occupant. He quickly noticed a boot with a narrow gambler's heel lying on the floor. The man was in a deep sleep, his snores irregular and loud like a snorting boar. Kinkead leaned over and removed a pistol from near the man's pillow and poked him with his rifle.

The startled man bounded wildly out of bed toward the center of the room. "What the hell?" As he tried to reach back for his pistol, he surrendered meekly when he saw the business end of a Henry rifle in his face. He identified himself as E. B. Parsons. He complained that he had done nothing wrong but was just a broke gambler come up to Loyalton to find a game.

Kinkead marched his man to a saloon down the street, where he showed his badge. He ordered the barkeep to bind his prisoner and keep him under guard until he returned the next day. Parsons, the New Hampshire born gambler, had been betrayed by his fancy boots.

Squiers was next. Tired but determined, Kinkead set out on a well-worn wagon road that would one day become California's Highway 49. It was two o'clock in the morning, and he had another long ride ahead of him. Snow flurries riding on the wintery west wind blasted his face; his tired horse struggled. He had learned to grab catnaps on horseback as a youngster, and it held him in good stead.

Reaching Sierraville, he tied his horse down the road and crept around behind Joe Squiers's house, where he hid in the willows. He knew he would have trouble taking brother John Squiers in the open. Surprise would be his ally.

At first light, a man walked out to the barn with a milk pail. Kinkead entered through the open kitchen door and looked into several rooms before seeing Squiers's familiar bearded face. Like Parsons, Squiers was in a coma-like sleep, the result of the wear of trekking over twenty miles. He had wrapped himself in a ragged patchwork quilt. His clothes and a whiskey bottle were at the foot of the bed, next to a shotgun.

Kinkead moved the shotgun to a corner and threw the clothes into the hall. He wakened Squiers with a nudge to the nose with his rifle. As Squiers groggily sat up, Kinkead put his finger across his lips. Prodding him with the rifle, he guided his half-naked captive outside before he let him dress.

As the man who had gone to the barn came around the corner of the house, Squiers yelled that he was being robbed. Three men in the house came out, and several early risers in the neighborhood gathered on the street. Kinkead pulled his coat open to show his badge and then lifted his rifle across his chest and patted it. He told the noisy, threatening crowd that he was an officer doing his duty, and that John Squiers was one of the men that had committed the train robbery at Hunter's two days earlier. Squiers denied the charge, saying the officer was out of his jurisdiction and had no right to make an arrest in California. The crowd, egged on by Joe Squiers, loudly agreed.

As matters began to turn for the worse, Kinkead noticed a man signal toward a wagon being hitched down the street. He rushed his prisoner to it and succeeded in getting away, with Squiers on the reins at gunpoint and his horse on a tether. Kinkead, sitting in the bed, ordered Squiers to head for Loyalton. There the bound Parsons was put on the wagon. Kinkead followed on horseback as they headed off to Truckee.

Although the robbery had taken place in Nevada, the Placer County sheriff wasn't about to let legal niceties get in the way of the jailing of men who had committed a railroad crime. The railroad, after all, was the reason Truckee existed. Kinkead telegraphed Nevada governor Henry G. Blasdel, asking him to request California governor Henry H. Haight to release the men for transport to Nevada.

The jailer took Kinkead to meet the prisoner hauled in the day before by Jim Burke and the deer hunters. It was the hapless, scared Irishman Jim Gilchrist. Until then a man of good reputation, he was nabbed shortly after committing his first crime. He had remained behind at the Sardine House because his feet were so swollen and blistered from the long hike with Squiers and Parsons that he couldn't get his boots on.

Deputies had put the press on Gilchrist, "sweating" him, as they called it. They told him he was facing twenty years hard time on the rock pile in Carson City. If he would give them the details of the train robbery, the law would go easy. Having felt the guilt rooted in his Irish Catholic upbringing from virtually the moment he joined the conspiracy, Gilchrist agreed to give a statement before a notary public. He provided the names of the men involved and gave the details of the planning and execution of the robbery.

California's governor quickly acceded to Governor Blasdel's extradition request. Squiers, Parsons, and Gilchrist were transported by train from Truckee to Reno under Kinkead's supervision. Forty-five minutes into the ride, Gilchrist pointed as the train passed the switch where the robbers had blocked the tracks. He talked the rest of the way as Kinkead took notes.

Based on Gilchrist's confession and Kinkead's lengthy report, warrants were issued for the arrests of John Chapman, Sol Jones, T. J. Cockerill, and Jack Davis. Three days after the robbery, Jones, Cockerill, and Chat Roberts, the saloon owner, were arrested in Long Valley.

After some persuasion in the "sweatbox" (Kinkead's term) and a promise of leniency, Jones admitted that he'd been involved. He led the officers to Red Rock where they dug up coins he and Cockerill had buried.

The train yard was put under watch. Three days after the robbery, John Chapman took an overnight passenger train from San Francisco to Truckee and a freight train to Reno the next morning. An officer assigned the watch arrested Chapman as he scurried between cars.

Chapman said he had never seen the "J. Enrique" telegram. He denied knowing anything about the robbery or having had any part in it. He protested that he had been in San Francisco looking for work for more than two weeks, and he produced rail ticket stubs and hotel receipts to prove it. His protestations were ignored.

In the meantime, based on the mounting evidence, the sheriff in Truckee sent a telegram to Virginia City, directing the arrest of Jack Davis. Davis was tracked down and taken by Washoe chief of police George Downey and constable Ben Lackey.

4
"The Trial Was a Memorable One in the Criminal Annals of Nevada"

On Jim Kinkead's death forty-two years later, his family found papers he had written describing his capture of the robbers and the ensuing trial. The trial, he wrote, "was a great legal battle, a memorable one in the criminal annals of Nevada."[3]

On November 23, 1870, Parsons, Chat Roberts, Gilchrist, Cockerill, Jones, Chapman, and Squiers were charged in a criminal complaint alleging that they had "committed the crime of robbery by feloniously and violently taking of and carrying away coin in the sum of about $40,000, the same being the property of Wells Fargo and Co. and taken by defendants as aforesaid from the transfer box in the Express car on the Central Pacific Rail Road."

Jack Davis was similarly charged in a separate complaint dated November 25, 1870. His lawyer was talking to prosecutors about a possible guilty plea and confession; a separate complaint would make it easier to cut a deal.

Chief judge C. N. Harris of Washoe County presided at the trial. Several prominent lawyers appeared for the prosecution and defense. W. M. Boardman, the Washoe County district attorney, represented the people, Thomas H. Williams appeared for Wells Fargo, and Kinkead's brother-in-law attorney general Robert M. Clarke represented the state of Nevada. Clarke would gain national recognition a few years later as the prosecutor of the perpetrators of a notorious robbery of the United States Mint in Carson City.

Jim Croffroth, a renowned San Francisco trial lawyer, represented the Central Pacific Railroad. Judge Thomas E. Haydon of Reno appeared as special counsel for robber John Chapman. The other defendants, with the exception of Jack Davis, were represented by William Webster of Washoe City, who was later to

---

[3] Kinkead's summary of the events was printed in the *Third Biennial Report* of the Nevada State Historical Society in 1913. A humble man, Kinkead did not identify himself in his writings as the person who had done the detective work and taken the risks that resulted in the quick capture of the robbers.

become the editor of the *Journal*, a Reno newspaper that has existed under various names to this day.

The trial was held in Washoe City, the seat of Washoe County.[4] The judge was robed in black. The lawyers wore the courtroom garb of the day: long black frock coats, high-collared white shirts, black string ties, and fancy boots. The *Territorial Enterprise* reported the start of the proceedings: "Court was called at 10 o'clock when the prisoners were brought into court, presenting a very fine appearance; in fact they were the finest appearing men in court—no disrespect to the attorneys and court."

The thorniest legal issue was raised by Judge Haydon, Chapman's attorney. The evidence was clear that Chapman was in San Francisco at the time of the alleged crime. Therefore, Haydon argued, the state of Nevada had no jurisdiction over him. If he could be tried anywhere it would have to be California, but he had committed no crime there. Haydon's motion to dismiss the charges against Chapman was taken under advisement by the court.

The motion shifted the burden to the prosecution. For Chapman to be tried in Nevada, prosecutors would have to produce evidence showing that he was part of a conspiracy and that the conspiracy had originated in Nevada.

Sol Jones was called as a witness for the prosecution. After identifying the men involved, he described his initial contact with Chapman, the meetings at Chat Roberts's place in Long Valley, the preparations at the tunnel on Peavine Mountain, and his part in stopping the train. He identified the "J. Enrique" telegram and pointed at Chapman as the one who had sent the wire from San Francisco.

Chapman shook his head as he glared at Jones.

Jim Gilchrist had been promised leniency. The promise was upgraded to full immunity on the condition that he testify truthfully as to what he knew and had previously told his captors. He did so, with his testimony focusing on the details of the robbery itself.

The investigation had shown that Chat Roberts, whose Long Valley saloon had been used as a meeting place by the conspirators, was never part of the planning and execution of the robbery. He was

---
[4] Reno became the county seat four months after the trial.

dismissed from the complaint and testified as to who attended the meetings at his place.

Kinkead took the oath and described how he arrested Parsons and Squiers. He also read from his notes of the details of the crime that Gilchrist had provided. A telegraph operator from San Francisco identified Chapman as the person who had sent the infamous telegram. Engineer Hank Small, his fireman, the train's express clerk, and law enforcement personnel gave corroborating testimony.

The evidence put John Chapman in the middle of the conspiracy and under the shadow of the laws of the state of Nevada. After a brilliant counterargument by attorney general Clarke, Judge Harris denied Chapman's attorney's motion contesting the court's jurisdiction.

As the evidence mounted, Jack Davis opted to plead guilty on the advice of his attorney, who had finally cut a deal. The prosecutors would recommend a light sentence if Davis would testify truthfully as a witness for the state. On the fourth day of trial, Davis entered a guilty plea and testified along the same lines as Jones and Gilchrist. He was immediately sentenced to ten years in the state prison. Absent his guilty plea, he was looking at a sentence of at least twenty years. As a result of subsequent events at the prison, the career robber would serve less than a year. A reporter wrote of Davis, "Chief of Police Downey conveyed him to [the prison in] Carson, and by two o'clock he was dressed in a suit of slingerland's best."

The attorneys for Squiers, Parsons, Davis, and Cockerill put friends of their clients on the witness stand to prove alibis. Cross-examination and sharp questioning by the judge undermined the veracity of their testimony.

After closing arguments, the judge instructed the jury on the elements of the crime of robbery. Three and a half hours later, the jury returned verdicts finding E. B. Parsons, John Chapman, Tilton Cockerill, and John Squiers "guilty as charged."

Sol Jones was sentenced the next day to five years in the state prison, the lightest sentence allowed by law. Parsons, Chapman, Cockerill, and Squiers received sentences ranging from eighteen to twenty-three years, with Squiers getting the longest term. It was Christmas Day 1870.

The court reporter wrote at the end of the trial: "[S]o ends the history of the most gigantic robbery ever perpetrated on the Pacific Coast. The most remarkable part of the history is the fact that within a space of five weeks the robbery was planned, executed, and all the parties arrested, $40,000 of the money recovered, all the prisoners tried and convicted and two of them are now in the state prison."

It was actually nearly seven weeks from the date of the robbery to the conclusion of the trial, and the planning had started two months earlier. But by any standard, it was a remarkably quick turn of events.

When the judge ruled that Nevada had jurisdiction to try him, John Chapman was certain he was going down for a long stretch. His reputation as a man who taught the word of the Lord had gotten him no sympathy. As the trial wore on, he was beleaguered with thoughts of rotting for decades in a foul prison surrounded by his co-conspirators, who, when all was said and done, he didn't particularly like. He resolved to take unauthorized leave of prison well before his time was served. He nodded knowingly at John Squiers sitting opposite him in the jail wagon and pointed out the window. Judging by the nod and smile coming back, he knew they were of like mind once again.

James A. Kinkead, who received the largest share of the reward, continued to distinguish himself in public service before going into business. He patented a milling technique and mined successfully on the Comstock for several years. He died on June 9, 1912.

Kinkead was the nephew of John H. Kinkead, who would become the third governor of Nevada (1879-1883) and later the first governor of the District of Alaska (1884-1885) on appointment by president Chester A. Arthur.

CHAPTER 4

The Break

1
The Prison

From an inmate's standpoint, the best that could be said about the Nevada State Prison in the state's early days was that it provided nourishment, a bunk, and, in a manner of speaking, clothing. When the court reporter at the robbery trial wrote that Jack Davis had been sent off to prison, he quipped that the robber would soon be "dressed in a suit of slingerland's best." He was referring to James S. Slingerland, in whose honor the prison uniforms were, one might say, affectionately named. Slingerland, a California native and former member of that state's legislature, had served as lieutenant governor during the second term (1866–1870) of Nevada's first governor, Henry G. Blasdel. As lieutenant governor, he was, by law, the ex officio warden of the state prison; hence the reference to "slingerland's best." Slingerland later became a deputy federal marshal. Soon after the trial and imprisonment of the train robbers, Slingerland was replaced as lieutenant governor by Frank Denver, who was on the November 1870 ballot with Lewis R. Bradley, who succeeded Blasdel as governor.

"Slingerland's best" was the standard prison uniform: coarse wool pants and shirt with three-inch-wide black-and-white horizontal stripes. It also included leg irons and the equally standard ball and chain.

Examples of the uniform used in the prison's early days are on display in the Nevada State Museum in Carson City.[1] Included with the display is a device that was meant to limit a prisoner's movement more effectively than a ball and chain, while leaving his hands free to work. It is a cruel-looking, L-shaped metal device that locked onto the lower leg and foot and prevented the ankle from bending. A man wearing the contraption would lumber along like Lon Chaney's Frankenstein.

---

[1] Since 1941, the state museum has been housed in the building that was once the United States Mint. With the Comstock Lode in full blossom, Congress in 1863 voted to establish a mint in Carson City. It opened in 1869 with Abraham Curry as its first superintendent. The sandstone used in its construction was quarried near the state prison. The brick was manufactured in nearby Genoa at the Adams Brick Works, which was owned and operated by the grandsons of John Quincy Adams.

The prison opened in 1862 when the Nevada Territorial Legislature authorized the purchase of the Warm Springs Hotel and the surrounding twenty acres from Abraham Curry, one of Carson City's more public-spirited citizens. Curry, who came to be known as "the father of Carson City," was appointed the prison's first warden while continuing to serve in the territorial legislature.

The original wooden prison building burned to the ground in 1867 and was replaced by one built from rock quarried near the prison grounds. The latter structure was in continual use until being decommissioned in 2012. The state capitol was constructed in part of rock from the quarries, as were several other state buildings.

The rock was quarried by prison inmates, whose labor generated income to fund prison operations. One hard-rock miner who had been sent up from Lander County commented that prison life "ain't so bad except for bustin' rocks in the quarry all day." He was one of the many Irishmen in the prison. He and his parents had likely emigrated during the potato famine that destroyed Ireland's primary food crop from the fall of 1845 through 1847.

Ireland's population dropped from eight million to five million during those and following years, due largely to starvation, disease, and emigration to the United States and Canada. The cause of the destruction of the potato crop, unknown at the time, was the fungus *Phytophthora infestans*, which literally turned the root crop to mush. British prime minister Robert Peel, an advocate of "market solutions" (a not-so-much-later version of Marie Antoinette's "let them eat cake" philosophy), refused to send relief. All the while, Ireland actually had plenty of food—eggs, cereals, meats—but almost all was designated for export, resulting in food riots and eventually the export of the country's people.

The experts, the priests, and the people blamed the famine on everything the imagination could conjure up: steam from trains, electricity, bad air, smells of unknown origin, bat guano fertilizers, even evil winds. The list was endless, but nothing was close to the truth. A million and a half people died of starvation and related diseases in the greatest loss of life in Europe since the Black Death (caused by bubonic plague) had killed an estimated twenty-five million in the fourteenth century.

Judging by his statement that things weren't so bad, the Irish prisoner must have appreciated regular meals, even if taken in confinement. He and his incarcerated countrymen probably spoke what linguists call Scots-Irish, a dialect that formed as lowland Scots emigrated to Northern Ireland—with help from the English king who by creating this movement for political purposes unwittingly abetted hundreds of years of 'troubles'— and assimilated the local language. Many left for the United States from the port at Belfast and, on reaching America, dispersed west or south through the Appalachians, where versions of the dialect are said to be spoken today.[2]

Economic depression was constant. Because Irish immigrants were a denigrated minority in some areas, including New York City, many couldn't find jobs in the East. The ranches and mines in the West needed men, Irish or not. Although the pay wasn't much, there was money enough for food and whiskey, and beds were available in bunkhouses and tent towns. Thousands came west working as laborers on the Union Pacific's section of the transcontinental railroad.

Most of the prisoners had committed the garden variety economic crimes of the day: stage robbery, burglary, larceny, and horse and cattle rustling. Some were in for murder, mayhem, or aggravated assault, crimes usually committed in mining camps during drinking binges. Mark Twain said that killing a man in Virginia City was a badge of honor. The toughest roustabouts had no compunctions in bragging how they "got their man." Rape, spousal abuse, racial violence, and juvenile crimes were rare, but shootings and shoot-outs among bad men and miners were regular events. There was one black man in the prison, but the rest were white; most were tattooed with India ink; many bore signs of bullet wounds and broken bones.

Except for a hanging judge in Elko County who meted out sentences excessive even for that wild territory, sentences weren't long by today's standards (with the notable exception of train robbery). One reason is the simple fact that people didn't live as long then as now and grew "old" more quickly, especially in prisons. If he didn't

---

[2] McCrum, et. al., p. 167.

die while incarcerated, a ten-year term could break a man's health and get him paroled, often to live out life as a harmless derelict.

The options on escape weren't good. The prison sits in a basin surrounded by mountains, with the Carson Range and the rugged Sierra Nevada looming to the west and southwest. The then-thriving mining towns of Gold Hill and Virginia City were a few miles northeast in the mountains, but an escapee arriving there would almost certainly be recognized. Reno was thirty miles north, hardly reachable without a horse, and a man in prison garb would stand out in the broad valleys between there and the prison. Except perhaps in the winter, a man could head west and survive in the Sierras where there was abundant water and food for one enterprising enough to live off the land. But it was a hundred miles west through those mountains to Hangtown, another fifty to Sacramento, and yet another ninety to San Francisco.

Other than a few fertile areas along the Walker and Carson Rivers, there was little to the east but barren mountains and Sonoran-like deserts, where potable water was scarce or, over large areas, nonexistent. There were a few small ranches and mining settlements to the south. The gold mining town of Aurora was a hundred miles in that direction, but it was supplied from Carson City, and news of an escape would get there in a day or two. A newcomer at any of the mining towns would not likely remain anonymous for long, and a rope and tree were always handy to take care of a miscreant.

Nonetheless, as is always the case with men in captivity, the lure of freedom was powerful, and escape was the only way to find it short of years on the rock pile. Led by the train robbers, a cabal formed in the summer of 1871 to plan an escape. On the fateful day, fully a third of the inmates would march out the gates.

2
The Plot

They're side by side in the quarry, hammering rocks. Charlie Jones walks up to John Chapman and testily says, "Chris-sakes, Chapman, why'd you let Roberts in? I heard he ran off and left another kid who was helping him knock off the Susanville stage. Left him wounded in the sagebrush and he bled out." Jones shakes his head. "How the hell can we trust him? He could just as well turn on us."

"Keep your voice down," Chapman says. "He's okay. Anyway, he figured out what's going on when he heard me pounding on the ceiling to see if there's a crawl space up there. I'll vouch for him."

They're talking about J. B. Roberts who was sent up from Washoe County for stage robbery. Just turned eighteen, he's the youngest man in the prison, the son of Chat Roberts, the saloon keeper from Long Valley who had hosted the train robbers. Slender, rosy-cheeked, unshaven and carrying a mop of blond hair, Roberts stands out among the more slovenly inmates.

Chapman waves for Leander Morton and Frank Clifford to follow as he walks to the latrine, a ditch behind canvas strung between poles. They stand concealed by the canvas.

"I told Jones the Roberts kid is in," Chapman says. "Are you working up the case? The men are anxious. They want details."

Leander Morton, a native of Ohio and a Civil War veteran, had been sentenced nine months earlier in Elko County to a thirty-year term for robbery. He has an Irishman's light hair, red whiskers, gray eyes, and a lopsided grin with front teeth missing from a punch in a barroom brawl. He's a small man, five feet four and weighing barely a hundred pounds.

"Okay, Roberts is in. I don't give a damn, long as I get out of here quick," Morton says, waving his arms around. He's pale even after working the quarry in the summer sun. His skin looks like it's been splattered with some kind of dirty-white talc. His mean-as-a-coyote reputation and his swagger make up for a diminutive physique. "Yes, we're on the case."

Frank Clifford, a twenty-eight-year-old Marylander, has made a living as a carpenter in the mills around hard-rock mines. He was sentenced in White Pine County a year and a half earlier to a ten-year term for assault and strong-armed robbery. He already has a date for a parole hearing.

Clifford says, "Chapman, the plan's done. We been working with Squiers. We'll lay it out for you tomorrow. We been watching how things run around here." He nods toward the guards on the hill above the quarry. "It'll be a go on a Sunday when most of 'em are outside the gates and the town is quiet."

"Give me the details tonight. I'll let Jones and Black know, and you can tell Burke and Parsons tomorrow," Chapman says. "The break is next Sunday?"

"Not next Sunday; two weeks. Seventeenth of September," Morton says. "Right after supper and Rollins or whoever the hell is guard captain that night comes in. We get him out of the way—kill the son of a bitch—and take his keys."

"A Sunday, a holy day," Chapman says with a smile. "I'll finally be able to tell the sinners in my Bible class that morning that sometimes you really can see through the dark glass Paul told the Corinthians about." He extends his arms to the heavens like a preacher addressing his flock.

"Hell ya talking about?" Morton says.

Chapman smiles and drops to a knee, head bent in mock prayer. "Thank you, Lord," he says. "Thank you."

"We got a crazy man here thinks he's the pope," Clifford says. "Damn! Stand up before the guards see you."

"We'll need all the help we can get from whatever god he's talking to," Morton says.

Chapman grabs Morton's hand. "The Lord tells us to 'rejoice in hope, be patient in tribulation.' That's Romans 12:12. Be firm, Morton. Your time of tribulation will soon be over."

The next day in the yard Clifford and Morton discuss the plan with Chapman and Parsons. "Chapman, you were right," Clifford says. "There's a crawl space in the ceiling above the mess hall and cells. Not a lot of headroom, but men can crawl through and get above the warden's rooms."

"We have to get the keys to the armory and get the guns. Warden has the keys," Morton says. "We put men in the ceiling, and when we give the signal, they drop into his rooms for a little surprise visit. He's always there on Sundays."

Morton stomps on his cigarette butt. "Clifford will lead the way on that end of things."

Clifford says, "Squiers will be the one to take out the guard when he comes in the dining hall. He'll kill him if he has to. Then we rush the armory from two ends, the warden's quarters and the main hall. We got Ryan passing out the guns."

"Ryan's in?" Chapman asks.

"He's damn happy about it too," Morton says. "Says he's going back to the old green sod."

Parsons butts in. "Seems like two weeks might be a little soon. We need to make sure we get it right. Maybe we should take our time, wait a bit, plan it out a little better."

"Hell you mean by 'wait'?" Morton sneers. "It's getting cold. I saw a dusting of white on the mountains the other morning. Wait any longer before getting out of here and there'll be snow. Then they'll track us easy and haul us back to this hellhole in no time."

"Morton's right. Sunday after next, Lord willing and it don't snow." Chapman, who is not a Catholic, mockingly crosses himself.

"Get off that religious stuff, Chapman." Morton spits as he says it. "I don't like to hear it."

Morton says, "Me and Burke and Charlie Jones and some others are heading south. Jones lived down in Bishop Creek once. He knows some people can help us. It'll take us a week to get there. Maybe less if we find us some horses."

Parsons points toward Prison Hill. "If we break after supper, it'll give us time to get around the hill, down the river, and across Mexican Dam by the time it gets dark. Then they'll have a hell of a time catching us. They can't track in the dark, and we can go a good piece by morning."

Morton says, "Jones knows where water is up in the Pine Nut Mountains. He says we should head for Sunrise Pass, but before we reach it, we cut south to Buckeye Creek and then angle off east for Wellington. He says stay off the main Sunrise road because that's a sure place where the law will think we'll head. There's a bunch of mines farther south and plenty of water."

"Clifford and I will head part of the way with you," Chapman says. "But we'll chance it by going over Sunrise instead of heading south with you. We want to get out east and then take the main road for Silver Peak down in lower Esmeralda. The pass is quicker."

Chapman draws in the dirt with a sledgehammer handle. "Once we get over the pass our group will cut through Smith Valley, diagonal over to the Walker River, and head on down past Walker Lake.

Once we're in Silver Peak, we're safe, and we've got work. The law is afraid to set foot there, and they're hard up for miners."

Chapman turns to walk away. He stops and looks back down at his map in the dirt. "We'll need to pick up some horses over in Smith, or we could die out in that Godforsaken country."

"Once you get past Walker Lake, you'll be facing a lot of desert," Morton says. "You won't make it all the way to Silver Peak without horses and water. If the sun don't get you the Paiutes will, and you won't like dyin' the way they like to do it." He makes a scalping motion and smiles broadly.

Parsons says, "George Roth is going with Chapman and me. He killed that Tibbs guy in Reno last year when he refused to pay up at the poker table. Tibbs damn well deserved it, the cheap son of a bitch." He points at Morton. "But we'll stick with you until you split off south."

"Roth says he isn't about to die in this place," Chapman says. "Smart German guy, and he can handle a gun with anyone."

"The ones besides us who knows everything is Squiers, Ryan, Jones, and Black," says Morton. "The Roberts kid only knows we're making plans. I also mentioned it to Burke, and he's thinking about it. He's driven team all the way down to Bishop Creek and Silver Peak and knows the country. Jones wants him along."

"A lot of men know something is coming," says Clifford. "But they don't know for sure, and they don't know when. Most won't know until we cut the hole in the ceiling after supper. We'll see how many follow us out."

"Okay," Morton says. "It's Sunday the seventeenth when we go. Soon's he takes out the guard, Squiers will signal to Clifford and the men in the crawl space. I don't much give a damn who follows as long as we get guns and get outside. Every man for hisself then."

Morton starts to walk away then looks back. "Good luck to you and your God," he says to Chapman. "After this thing's over, I hope I never hear that preachin' again."

"May the Lord bless you, Morton. First Corinthians tells us He will provide the way of escape, that you may be able to endure it." Chapman deliberately misquotes the passage.

"I ain't aware of no 'Lord' around here," says Morton. "Leastwise ain't none that's gonna waste any time on me."

3
The Escape

Volney Rollins checked his sidearm and buttoned his coat against a cold draft as he walked down the concrete hallway toward the dining area. His last duty was to secure the prisoners. It had been a long day, and he just wanted to sit in front of a fire with his family.

I'll lock 'em up for the night, and I'm out of here. It was the last thought he remembered from that day.

Some three dozen inmates were assembled in the dining hall, the conspirators among them milling about as nervous as wild horses before a thunderstorm. It had come time for Rollins, the captain of the guard, to get them back in their cells. As he unlocked and opened the iron door, a bottle swung by John Squiers smashed into the top of his head, and a slungshot hit him above the left eye, slashing his forehead to the bone. Several prisoners rushed him wildly as he sank to the floor. One grabbed his sidearm and others were about to assault him again, but just as they reached him, Pat Hurley, a small, dark Irishman serving five years for an Ormsby County robbery, made his way through the mob, pulled the guard by his coat collar and hair into a cell, and slammed the door. Rollins slept through the ensuing battle, owing his life to a little man who, judging by the tattoo of a vase of flowers on his forearm, had a soft spot in his heart.

Thus began the largest prison break in the history of the country. It happened on September 17, 1871, a bleak Sunday evening when strong winds sweeping off the western mountains had cast a dirty, blinding pall over the valley. The bitter-cold winds were harbingers of an early winter. The prison wasn't a pleasant place for even the most hardened of men to spend a winter, and talk of the coming cold was a dreadful refrain among the inmates.

The prisoners had armed themselves with a variety of crude weapons, including reinforcement bars and knives of their own making. Some carried slungshots made of rocks or hunks of metal sewn into socks tied to their wrists.

A hole had been cut in the ceiling and several men were waiting in the crawl space. When Squiers rapped on the ceiling from below, they moved quickly to a point above the warden's quarters. Frank

Clifford was in front. They were after the keys to the armory and the gates, and it didn't matter who stood in their way.

Frank Denver, the lieutenant governor, was the warden. Denver's wife, his six-year-old daughter Jennie, and his mother-in-law were having supper in the dining room of the warden's quarters. They were aghast as a sledgehammer broke through the ceiling and men in convict garb dropped into the room. Denver, who heard the ruckus from downstairs, appeared with his pistol drawn, but he was immediately overwhelmed and struck a vicious blow to the back of the head. As he pitched forward, a slungshot opened a three-inch gash in his forehead; blood blinded him as he sank to the floor. A prisoner grabbed his pistol and shot him in the midsection.

Bob Deadman, a trustee serving life for a Virginia City murder, had followed Denver up the stairs. He grabbed a chair and went hell-bent after the prisoners. Newspapers reported that Deadman managed to knock five men to the floor and another "over the balustrading and down the stairs" before he was knocked senseless and left for dead.

The break had been timed perfectly. The guard shift was reduced on Sundays, and most of the few guards on duty were doing checks on the outer reaches of the property before nightfall.

The mob left the two women and the little girl unharmed as Clifford led the charge downstairs to the armory. Initial accounts said the convicts helped themselves to two Henry rifles, four double-barreled shotguns, five six-shooters, and over two thousand rounds of ammunition. In fact, more weapons were seized, both from the armory and, later, from downed guards.

Thomas Ryan, a scarred, red-headed Irishman sent up from Lander County for burglary and escape, had the job of checking the weapons records in Denver's office. He noticed a Henry rifle was missing. A newspaper account stated that when Ryan shouted upstairs to ask where the rifle was, Denver appeared on the balcony, six-shooter in hand, daring Ryan to come and get it. The story was false. Denver was lying in his living room, shot through the gut and bleeding profusely from a head wound. Ryan found the rifle under a coat in the office.

Heavily armed prisoners burst out of the cell block and headed for the gates. In the yard, F. M. Isaacs, a guard from Gold Hill, confronted them and fired away with a pistol. A description of Isaacs's bravery that day is reminiscent of the flowery prose in correspondents' reports of the supposed heroics of General George Armstrong Custer. Custer would die five years later at Little Big Horn at the hands of Indians led by the great chiefs Sitting Bull and Crazy Horse.

> Isaacs stood like a stone column, firing steadily into the motley crowd and receiving volley after volley with the coolest indifference. A ball passed through his right knee, breaking it, and lodged in the rear of the left knee. At this Isaacs straightened himself up, threw the weight of his body on the left and only unbroken leg, and fired again. By this time the armed desperadoes at whom he was firing were almost within striking distance of him, were steadily approaching and as steadily firing at him with 6-shooters. Another shot hit the heroic Isaacs in the arm and sent him to earth. The prisoners seized his pistol, but out of sheer admiration of heroic courage spared his life.[3]

Isaacs was a brave man and as heroic as anyone involved in the affray. But it's unlikely he was spared out of admiration for his courage. He was down with grave wounds, having been shot in the hip as well as the knees, and was unable to rise to protect himself. Disarmed, he was no threat, and the fleeing escapees paid no mind to him.

As Isaacs was facing mortal danger, convict William Russell, a burglar from Storey County, was looking for a target. He spotted Mrs. Denver peering through curtains from the second story parlor of the warden's quarters. She was looking for her daughter, who had disappeared. It was reported that the ball Russell fired passed within inches of the woman's head, between her and a "gentleman visitor" who stood with her watching the conflict. The "gentleman" must have been her mother, since Denver and Deadman, the trustee, were down, and there were no other men in the warden's quarters.

Guard John Newhouse burst into the yard just as his friend Isaacs went down. He told investigators he thought his first shot had

---

[3] *Daily State Register*, September 19, 1871.

seriously wounded train robber E. B. Parsons. He was rendered senseless by a slungshot blow to the back of the head before he could get off more rounds.

An unarmed Slovakian prison guard from Carson City named Perasich heard the sounds of battle and raced to the nearby Warm Springs Hotel, a favorite watering hole of the guards. He grabbed a five-shooter from behind the bar, rushed back to the entry to the prison yard, and began firing. He reported later he was certain that least three shots took effect, as he saw men "squirm and stagger." Within a minute, he was shot in the left hip, the ball deflecting down through the groin and lodging between the femoral artery and thigh bone. Had the ball struck the artery, Perasich, who survived his wounds, would have been dead in short order.

Matthew Pixley, the proprietor of the hotel, armed himself and ran after Perasich. Prisoners were in the guard room firing into the yard at Newhouse and Perasich. Pixley rushed pell-mell up to a window and raised his pistol to fire. Charlie Jones, a ringleader of the escape, whirled and fired a Henry rifle through the window. The bullet penetrated two panes of glass and struck Pixley below the eye. He was dead before he hit the ground, his blood and brains splattered along the wall and yard.

C. W. Burgesser, Pixley's barkeep, grabbed a rifle and followed his boss headlong into the fray, meeting a hair-breadth escape with his life. The *Daily State Register* reported that a "ball shaved close by each ear, and a third shot struck his pantaloons in the front of the crotch and tore away the whole seat of both pants and drawers."

Newspapers had kind words for another "guard," a little Frenchman whose name was not at first known, who "fought heroically to the last and escaped without a scratch." It was said that he rushed through the crowd, dealing many telling blows "regardless of the shower of shots that whistled about him and cut his clothes to shreds."

During the heat of the battle, the Frenchman noticed Warden Denver's panicked daughter running through the yard. He "rushed out in the leaden storm, seized the little girl and started running with her along the prison building toward the west gate with the intention of putting her [out of harm's way]." As he ran through a hail of gunfire with the girl, he saw a young woman "running toward the prison door, to reach which she would have to pass in front of four guns belching streams of fire from the windows. The gallant little Frenchman, having removed the child from danger, dropped her and seized the woman, thus saving her from instant death."

The Frenchman then rushed back to the battle scene where he encountered C. W. Burgesser, the hotel bartender who had managed to fight on despite the loss of the rear end of his pantaloons. He yelled to Burgesser, "Here, barkeep, help me take this man out of danger!" With bullets plowing up the ground, the two men rushed the yard and carried the grievously wounded Isaacs to safety. The Frenchman turned to return to the scene, but Burgesser grabbed his arm and convinced him that the prisoners, having seen what he had done, would surely kill him. He agreed and let Burgesser lock him in a room in the hotel.

It turned out that the Frenchman the newspapers identified as a guard was a convict himself, as Burgesser knew. His name was Edmond Goyette. He was serving a lengthy term for assault with intent to do great bodily harm during a brawl in Virginia City.

It was mayhem. The prisoners, some letting out Civil War battle cries, ran, stepped, pushed, and shoved over and around the fallen guards. Twenty-nine of them made it over the walls or through the gates and ran off in all directions, hell-bent on freedom.

A man in a buggy who heard the noise of the battle rushed back to Carson City's main street and alerted authorities. Sheriff Swift and a dozen armed men immediately left for the prison but were too late to prevent the escape of any man who chanced a run for it.

It was reported that twenty-two of the escapees, marching two abreast, turned east toward the river. Like many exaggerated reports written in the next few days, that was not true. The men simply scattered. Several who headed toward the Sierras slipped through the outlying regions of Carson City without incident. One of them followed the Carson River upstream for miles. He was captured without incident two days later, basking in a pool at David Walley's Hot Springs near Genoa in Douglas County. "A warm bath was all I wanted," he said.

A group of stragglers in prison garb was seen at dusk on a ridge across the Carson River, a few miles southeast of the prison. Lawmen said they would be captured before daylight.

The state militia headquartered in Virginia City was called out by the governor's office; troops arrived by special train three hours later. The state armory was opened, and citizens were deputized and sent to the prison to guard against another escape attempt or an attack by the insurgents.

Victory in the battle went to the escapees. Frank Clifford, who suffered a flesh wound from a shot by Warden Denver in the first minutes of the battle, was the only injured convict. In light of the fact that dozens if not hundreds of rounds were fired by guards—and by Denver and Burgesser and Goyette—it's remarkable that no other prisoners were injured.

Carson City's *Daily State Register* and Virginia City's *Daily Territorial Enterprise* carried identical accounts of the battle with datelines of September 19, 1871. The twenty-nine escapees were described as being "as desperate a gang of villains as ever faced the sun."

Not a single escapee was captured the day of the escape. For weeks newspapers would condescendingly criticize the National Guard generals, the sheriffs, the warden and deputy warden, and the leaders of the newly armed citizen militias. Much of the criticism was well founded, given that all came away empty-handed.

Reports days later were that prisoner Frank Clifford had been fatally wounded by Lieutenant Governor Denver in the warden's quarters. Goyette thought he heard him say, "I'm dying" as he left through the gate. Clifford's wound, however, was inconsequential. There were equally erroneous reports that train robber E. B. Parson had been badly wounded and that eight other prisoners had been shot.

A *Daily State Register* reporter who accompanied investigators described what he saw two days after the battle.

> At the prison, the scene was appalling, even yesterday morning, when everything was still as the grave. Blood—great blotches and pools of human gore—greeted the eye everywhere; along the porch of and in the hotel, on the

main gateway, over the rubble stones of the inner walk, on the prison porch, door steps, window and door sills and facing, wall coating, walls, bolts bars, beds, floors, stairs and even the little green shade trees and the green grass of the front yard were stained with blood. Everywhere marks of the heroic struggle of the few brave guards against overwhelming numbers of superiorly armed desperadoes were visible.

4
The Aftermath:
"Many a Tear Will Water the Soil that Covers His Remains"

Governor Lewis R. Bradley announced rewards for the capture of the escapees. Their descriptions were widely published and they were sought by lawmen and citizens far and wide.

The deputy warden, who had run off to sound the alarm as the escape began, was publicly vilified and forced to resign. He was branded a coward for not returning to the action. Lieutenant Governor Denver thought himself a hero deserving of approbation, but his reputation was to fade quickly as the investigations and name-calling began.

The rumor mill churned with speculation that the escapees had been aided from the outside. One editor wrote: "Circumstantial evidence now renders the presumption great and the conclusion almost irresistible, that the prisoners expected and did actually receive moral and material aid from outsiders." It was claimed, for example, that the lock on the door of the armory had been loosened so an iron bar could be crammed in to pry the door open. None of the allegations were substantiated during the ensuing investigations. In fact, the prisoners had gotten access to the armory with a key taken from the warden's office.

The little Frenchman Goyette, the heroic prisoner who was first thought to be a guard and who had saved the life of the lieutenant governor's daughter, was pardoned a month later. The Board of Pardon Commissioners looked into the violent fracas that had originally landed him in prison for severely beating a man. The board found that but for the state of excitement in Virginia City at the time, where the city fathers had instituted a crackdown on excessive drinking and barroom violence, Goyette would have been found guiltless on the ground of self-defense. The board said that on the day of the battle at the prison, "young Goyette time and again placed himself in the most imminent peril to save women and children from the storm of bullets that whistled about them, and finally seized poor Isaacs who had been twice shot down and bore him outside the walls."

A few days after the battle, it was reported that Goyette's arm, broken during the fight, had been set and that he was progressing well. He received state-sponsored medical treatment due to his heroics at the prison.

Newspapers also touted the story of Bob Deadman, the trustee who had helped Denver during the fight in the warden's quarters. "His heroic conduct doubtless saved the life of the Lieutenant Governor and was the theme of universal praise in this city as soon as it became known." The board pardoned Deadman and restored him to full citizenship. It was reported that "this action of the Board will meet with the hearty approbation of every good citizen in the State." Deadman got the penultimate reprieve, since he was serving a life term for murder.

John Newhouse, the guard who had been struck on the head with a slungshot, "had a stiff neck for the first time yesterday, but the wound is not thought to be dangerous." That report came two days after the battle.

Captain of the guard Volney Rollins, the battle's first victim, returned to duty the day after the break, albeit with an aching, bandaged head. A member of a prominent, early day Eagle Valley family, he provided important information about prison operations during the ensuing investigations, the reports of which prompted the legislature to take corrective measures.

Lieutenant Governor Denver was in serious condition. A week after the battle, the Carson newspaper reported that the gunshot to his midsection was troubling him considerably from hip to back, "owing to the fact that suppuration had started." "Dr. Lee sluiced out the wound ... with carbolic acid, and took out several pieces of cloth which had been forced in ahead of the ball." Suppuration was the discharge of pus that indicated an infection. The cleansing of the wound was intensely painful, but afterward Denver was said to be "gradually approaching convalescence."

A week later, Denver was improved; it was said he would "shortly be about again." On October 6, almost three weeks after he was wounded, he was convalescing well but still unable to leave his bed. Given the nature of his wounds, Denver was fortunate his physicians had been able to prevent serious infection from setting in.

A week after the report that he was unable to leave his bed, he was "around again, looking exceedingly well; rather pale, but for a man who has within a month received wounds severe enough to kill an ox—he is certainly better than could be expected." He eventually recovered and served out his term as lieutenant governor.

The battle for life on the part of guard F. M. Isaacs is a study in the treatment of gunshot wounds before antibiotics. As chronicles of the Civil War note, in the case of a person who at first appeared to recover from his wounds, subsequent death was almost always caused by infection, by gangrene in most cases. Gangrene is a life-threatening condition that occurs when a mass of tissue dies (necrosis). It is often accompanied by severe pain.

Reports on Isaacs, who was known throughout northern Nevada, were carried in nearly every issue of Carson City's *Daily State Register* and the *Reno Daily Crescent* during the month following the battle. Two days after he was wounded, a report was that he "will certainly lose his right leg above the knee, and the chances are decidedly against his recovery." A few days later, it was reported that he had begun to sink fast. Small hopes were entertained for his recovery.

But the ensuing prognosis was positive. A week after he was wounded, he "was better yesterday than at any time since the wounds were received. The wound passing from the left hip to the right thigh troubles him but little, the worst wound being that of the right knee, the bone of which is shattered. The swelling had subsided in the leg yesterday morning, and the wound was suppurating freely." His body had begun the healing process; his spirits were high. His attending physicians were doing excellent work.

The next day's report, however, was distressing: "Mr. Isaacs is in a very low condition, his main attendant, Judge Wells, informs that the wounds are doing as well as could be expected and that the medical men say that vital power in the patient is all that is needed in working a cure."

Isaacs began to exhibit symptoms (pain, discoloration, numbness, nausea) of infection in the knee wound. On October 2, 1871, two weeks after he was wounded, Dr. Lee of Carson City and Dr. Webber and Dr. Collins of Virginia City amputated his right leg. The thigh was cut above the knee, which was found to have been completely shattered. The bone of the lower leg had been blown open for a distance of four inches. The doctors found that gangrene had set in and reported that the amputation had been performed none too soon. Isaacs, they said, had borne up heroically, "being but partially under the influence of chloroform." They speculated that if he survived another day he would recover.

As it was performed before the development of anesthetics, the horror of amputation is difficult to comprehend. The criterion was survivability. The work with keen-edged knives and saws was relatively quick, but completion of the operation was slowed as arteries were tied off and some kind of closed stump fashioned in an attempt to stave off infection.

Isaacs was not given enough chloroform to render him unconscious. Doctors were careful in its administration because it was known to cause cardiac arrest. Morphine was apparently not available, although it had created thousands of addicts during the Civil War a few years earlier. To the extent pain medications were available, they were not often administered after the fact due to the belief they would inhibit the body's ability to recover. That anyone survived, even for a day, the kind of operation Isaacs endured is testament to human courage, yet Civil War records show that survival was not uncommon.

On October 5, Isaacs was improving. As of October 6, he was said to be "lingering and still low but his condition is thought to be favorable."

On October 8, a relatively favorable prognosis came: "[H]e was much better yesterday ... [S]trong hopes are now entertained that he will be restored to health."

On the morning of October 12, the *Daily State Register* reported that the "condition of Mr. Isaacs has greatly improved within the last two days, and without some unforeseen change for the worse he will probably recover." The key words were "unforeseen change." That night Isaacs took a severe turn for the worse.

On October 14, the *Daily State Register* reported that "we expected yesterday to be under the painful necessity of this morning announcing the death of F. M. Isaacs, the brave prison guard who lost a leg and was otherwise dangerously wounded in the late break; but he was alive when we went to press." Isaacs had sunk so quickly, then, that he was expected to die on October 13. He did in fact die after press time, in the premidnight hours of October 13, 1871.

Oddly enough, the October 14 edition of the *Reno Daily Crescent* reported that Isaacs "has been reported as dying so many times that folks begin to think there is no die in him. Too much interest is felt in recovery for him to go now. His medical attendant … said, on being asked his opinion, that no one but the Almighty knew anything about him. Mr. Isaacs has nerves of steel and a constitution of iron." Isaacs was dead when that edition hit the streets.

The inquest was held on October 14, the day after this death, which indicates that his passing had been expected long enough to summon a coroner's jury. Infection was determined to be the immediate cause of death.

Judge Thomas Wells, who had overseen his care, was "so overpowered by the labor and anxiety of attending Mr. Isaacs that he was for a time completely prostrated, and for some time considered in a dangerous condition." He was confined to his room and did not recover in time to attend the funeral.

A coroner's jury found that barkeep Matthew Pixley had been killed by weapons in the hands of prisoners Charles Jones and Thomas Flynn. Since only one shot hit Pixley, both men couldn't have killed him. However, Isaacs stated before his death that both men had fired at Pixley simultaneously, so it was impossible to say which man actually caused the death. Therefore the coroner's jury declared both to be responsible for the killing and the rest of the escapees to be accessories to the crime. The matter could be sorted out later by a trial jury.

Thomas Flynn, alias Matthew Rafferty, had been sent up from White Pine County for larceny. He was captured in Rocklin, near Sacramento, three weeks after the escape. On being informed he was charged with the murder of Pixley, he claimed he wasn't close to the window where Pixley was shot. He said Charlie Jones shot Pixley and that Jones and Leander Morton did the most effective shooting.

Within two months, eighteen of the recaptured escapees, including Flynn, were indicted for the murders of Isaacs and Pixley. The trial for the Isaacs murder commenced on November 23, 1871, in the Ormsby County District Court in Carson City before Judge C. N. Harris, who had presided over the trial of the train robbers a year earlier in Washoe County. Attorney general Robert M. Clarke, who had also appeared at the robbery trial, assisted the prosecution.

The *Reno Crescent* reported that the prisoners "were half starved when brought [to the county jail] from the Prison, having been regaled with bread and water since their recapture." But once in the jail, Sheriff Swift started "feeding them on good substantial grub, and they are getting to look sleek and hearty."

Astute courtroom observers predicted that convictions of murder in the first degree as alleged would be impossible to obtain. The indictment was said to be defective and should have been quashed.

On November 27, the jury found the convicts "not guilty as charged in the indictment." Among them were the train robbers John Squiers, John Chapman, and E. B. Parsons. The jurors relied on eyewitness testimony that Charlie Jones and Leander Morton, who weren't present at the trial, were the killers. The *Daily State Register* observed that "the prisoners were overjoyed, and, as they pinched, munched, nudged, shoved and struck each other, there was a kind of 'oh no, it ain't us' sort of expression on their countenances."

A reporter for the *Reno Crescent* wrote that the men were returned to the state prison after the trial "and will languish in dark cells and feast on bread and water until the Ides of March" unless the attorney general should relent and allow them regular prison fare. "If I wanted to ship a crew for a pirate vessel, I would offer those eighteen convicts the highest monthly wages ever heard of."

As a consequence of the Isaacs verdict, the indictment for the murder of Pixley was determined to be defective and was not reissued. Prosecutors knew that the only person who could now be charged with the reasonable expectation of a guilty verdict was Charlie Jones, but he had not been captured.

Pat Hurley, the little Irish prisoner with a tattoo of flowers on his arm, had saved the life of the captain of the guard by pulling him out of harm's way as the breakout started. After the fray, Hurley set out on a remarkable odyssey that shows the pluck, guile, and desperation of these men.

After scurrying through the prison gate, Hurley struck out south along the Carson River, alone and on foot. He skirted Carson City and headed west into the Sierras. He followed the wagon road over Spooner Summit, a half-mile elevation gain, and then down to the shore of Lake Tahoe. He walked halfway along the twenty-mile-long lake to the north shore and crossed into California. He finally reached the railroad town of Truckee, not far from where the Donner Party had been marooned little more than two decades earlier. All told, it was a walk of over forty miles, most of it at night.

Still in prison garb and with a six-shooter taken from the prison armory tucked in his waistband, Hurley was treated to a few whiskeys in a Truckee bar by amused, drunken railroad workers who marveled at his story. He strong-armed one of them out behind the bar and took five dollars. He scoured the back alleys and found an old coat and some pants that he thought "belonged to some mason."

Hurley took the Central Pacific train from Truckee over Donner Pass to Colfax, a small railroad town tucked away in the forest. After working up a stake playing cards, he rode on to Petaluma in Sonoma County north of San Francisco Bay, where he won seventy-five dollars playing poker during Fair Week.

He backtracked to Vallejo on the North Bay and hung out at the shipyard. Unable to find work, he took a ferry to San Francisco and a stage to Monterey, where he spent his time in the bars and bordellos. When arrested in a saloon back in San Francisco, he told his captors that when the money was gone his "idea was to go to Vallejo and ship out on a man-of-war."

About the time Hurley was taken back to prison, train robber John Squiers was captured in nearby Six Mile Canyon in a mining tunnel. It was the canyon where Squiers had pulled off an infamous stage robbery a decade earlier to raise money for a trip home to Connecticut. A Henry rifle was found in the tunnel. A reward of $300 was paid for his capture and $200 for an escapee found with him.

Matthew Pixley's funeral was held in Carson City. Long before the corpse arrived, the church was filled, the fire companies had turned out, "and a more solemn procession never marched through Carson." The good Reverend C. G. Allen "delivered a very impressive and appropriate discourse. The choir was superb, and all the honor that could be paid was shown to the departed hero." Pixley was "one of the noblest young men in the country." He was polite and generous, it was said, with a new marriage opening a happy life before him. The elders felt as though a son had been lost.

The Carson City newspaper reported Reverend Allen's homage to young Pixley:

> We know of no bad habits poor Mat. possessed, although raised in this wild western country and full of high courage and buoyant spirit; he was always gentlemanly and respectful; slow to anger; firm in friendship; in fact, in every attribute a man. Sincerely do I console with his sorrowing young wife and relatives. Many and many a tear has and will water the soil that covers his remains. Truly a hero has gone.

Pixley, born in North Carolina, was murdered two days short of his twenty-fourth birthday. He was laid to rest in Carson City's Lone Mountain Cemetery. His wife, Ina Mills, was buried beside him many years later.

The funeral of prison guard F. M. Isaacs was held in Virginia City on Sunday, October 15, 1871, four weeks after the prison battle. The Masonic Fraternity conducted the rites. The day was filled with pageantry, like a solemn Fourth of July. There were members of fraternal organizations, representatives of the guard corps, law enforcement personnel, state and local officials, and a thousand ordinary citizens. The speeches were grand, and afterward the saloons came alive with toasts in remembrance of a man who in the last weeks of his life had endured a living hell.

The day was reminiscent of Mark Twain's description of the funeral of his Virginia City icon Buck Fanshaw.

> The obsequies were all that "the boys" could desire. Such a marvel of funeral pomp had never been seen in Virginia. The plumed hearse, the dirge-breathing brass bands, the closed marts of business, the flags drooping at half mast, the long, plodding procession of uniformed secret societies, military battalions and fire companies, draped engines, carriages of officials, and citizens in vehicles and on foot, attracted multitudes of spectators to the sidewalks, roofs, and windows, and for years afterward, the degree of grandeur attained by any civic display in Virginia was determined by comparison with Buck Fanshaw's funeral.[2]

Isaacs was thirty-nine years old when he died. He was survived by his wife and two children. His obituary is still on Nevada's Officer Down Memorial Page.

Although his wounds healed and he eventually resumed his duties, the saga of lieutenant governor Frank Denver continued. Legislators were decidedly unhappy with the circumstances of the prison escape, the deaths that ensued, and operations at the prison generally. There were public charges of "terrible mismanagement"; that "something is wrong" in the administration of the prison; that the prison board was to blame by diminishing the number of guards in the name of economy; that the board was composed of "incompetent men on account of political bias."

The *Reno Crescent* took up the cry:

> It is to be hoped that our Lieutenant Governor will profit by the severe lesson he has received, and in the future maintain a stricter surveillance over these unmitigated

---
[2] Twain, p. 177.

scoundrels, selecting his guards and deputy with more discretion, to the end that expense may be saved to the State, and brave men's lives may not be endangered through the treachery and cowardice of incompetent men.

Despite his heroics in battling the prisoners in his quarters, Denver became a marked man, a scapegoat by his reckoning. A new law targeted him by requiring that the warden have professional law enforcement credentials. It also changed the makeup of the prison's governing board and placed ultimate responsibility with the governor.

Lacking law enforcement training, Denver wouldn't be qualified to remain as warden after the law's effective date of April 1, 1873. In response to political pressure, however, Governor Bradley ordered Denver to vacate his post two weeks early. Denver adamantly and publicly refused. He argued that the legislation was not yet effective, so for him to relinquish his duties would be unlawful. A court would likely have agreed with him; nonetheless, he backed down and resigned when confronted with state militiamen and artillery sent to the prison by the angry, embarrassed governor. He kept a low profile for the two years remaining in his term as lieutenant governor. He died in 1875 at age forty-eight, shortly after the end of his term.

Deputy Warden Zimmerman, who gave the alarm as the prison break unfolded, did not return to the scene. For that he was ridiculed and driven from office. "It is said that the Deputy Warden … who so bravely ran away … has concluded to resign his position," said the *Reno Crescent*. "He will be presented with a medal by the citizens in token of their appreciation of his discretion, which is allowed to be the better part of valor." He was "a fine appearing man, so it would have been a fearful outrage to have marred his human form divine."

Of the train robbers, Chapman, Parsons, and Squiers were back in prison within days. Cockerill would be captured two hundred miles south in Esmeralda County two months after the prison break. Although they faced the full terms of their decades-long sentences plus added time for escape, with the exception of Parsons, they were out on parole within eleven years.

After his parole Squiers moved to California, where he was convicted of jury tampering and sentenced to five years in San Quentin State Prison. Years later, James H. Kinkead, the lawman who had led the capture of the train robbers, said of Squiers: "A few years ago he was a spectator at the Gans-Nelson fight in Goldfield. He is now a gray-haired, decrepit old man, who, if still living, is too old to do much damage in this world." [3]

Train robbers Jack Davis and Sol Jones had cooperated with the prosecution during the robbery trial and were serving far shorter sentences than the other robbers. Since they refused to participate in the prison break and even helped in the cleanup, they were granted early parole dates. Jones disappeared into history.

Davis, however, continued his quest for easy money. On September 3, 1877, he and two confederates attempted to hold up a stage traveling between the Nevada mining camps of Eureka and Tybo. As the robbers appeared on the road with arms drawn, guards on the stage immediately opened fire with double-barreled shotguns. As Kinkead told it, "Eugene Blair, a shotgun messenger, got the drop on him [Davis] and riddled his chest with buckshot, making a truly 'good Indian' of him."[4] Davis was lying facedown on the dusty road, beard and clothes caked with blood, when the coroner arrived to carry his remains off to a potter's field.

Train robber E. B. Parsons may have eventually made it back to his long lost sweetheart in his native New Hampshire. After being recaptured after the prison break, he took part in yet another break. Arrested again, he fled from a holding cell at the Ormsby County

---

[3] See Kinkead at p. 115 of the Nevada State Historical Society 13th Biennial Report. Joe Gans, the "Old Master," and Battling Nelson, the "Durable Dane," fought in Goldfield, Esmeralda County, Nevada on Labor Day 1906. The legendary fight was featured on the front pages of many of the country's dailies. The unshaded ring was outdoors on a scorching-hot day. The fight ended in round 42 when Nelson was disqualified for a punch to Gans's groin. It was the longest boxing match ever fought under the Marquis of Queensbury rules. The men battled for 2 hours and 50 minutes before a crowd of thousands. Original newspaper clippings describing the fight still adorn the walls of Goldfield's oldest saloon, the Sante Fe, where many of the spectators gathered to relive the match after it ended.
[4] Ibid.

jail in Carson City and was never found. Thus, to paraphrase New Hampshire's motto, the man whose pointy gambler's boots had led to the capture of the train robbers, lived free and didn't die.

The reporter at the robbery trial noted how remarkable it had been that within the space of five weeks the robbery had been planned, executed, all the parties arrested, the money recovered, and the perpetrators sent to prison. Now it could be added that, within a year, several of the robbers had been instrumental in planning and carrying out the largest prison break in the country's history, had taken part in a murderous prison rampage, and had escaped and been recaptured. It could be further added that all this precipitated a political firestorm that brought down the prison administration and led to significant changes in Nevada correctional policy.

As much of this transpired, Robert Morrison, a young merchant who lived nearly two hundred miles south in Mono County, California, was planning his wedding. Thanks to the train robbers and prison plotters, Morrison's fiancée would be a "widow" before she could wed.

CHAPTER 5

A Murder Most Gruesome

1
The Devil Charlie Jones

*C*harlie Jones, the convict who would play a pivotal part in the fateful events that followed the prison break, had made a stupid mistake by killing a man in a drunken brawl. It got him ten years in prison. But he wasn't a stupid man. Letters from his cell to one Mrs. Luna Hutchison of Bishop Creek showed him to be quite intelligent. His saga makes one wonder what he could have done with his life under different circumstances.

Mrs. Hutchison, a member of the National Prison Association, was dedicated to prison reform. "If an angel was put into some prisons," she had written as a member of the association, "he would become a devil in a few years … [N]or will the world ever be made better by the taking of life for life, as the experiment has long been tried and failed in suppressing crime, for it is proved where the death penalty is most prevalent crime and murder more abound, but are found to decrease with its abrogation."

After the Nevada prison break and after suspicion had been directed toward her because of her correspondence with Jones, she gave the letters Jones had written to her to the Bishop newspaper with liberty to publish them "if I am to be subject to suspicions of which I am wholly innocent." She remained defiant. Whether she gave aid and comfort to Jones after his escape was never determined.

The first letter was dated November 6, 1871. The date was probably the newspaper's printing error; from its text, it's clear the letter had been written earlier in the year. Moreover, by November 6, Jones had been on the run for weeks and had not been captured. The letter in part reads thus:

> Mrs. L. Hutchison: My dear friend—your kind and interesting letter … made me feel as though I was not entirely forgotten, and had at least some few friends left in the outside world. [The letter] not only smooths [*sic*] the roughness of prison life, but casts a ray of hope over the despondency of a prisoner's feelings.

I must say to your remark, "You are certainly free from the fret and cares of what you shall wear," etc., is quite consoling and *almost* makes a man satisfied with his confinement ... but I would much rather be out at work and earning food and raiment by the sweat of my brow ... than be incarcerated here. [F]reedom is inate [*sic*] in the breast of both man and beast. Young as I am, it is worse than if I were old and on the shady side of life and fast nearing the grave, for then the mere substance of life would be all that would be required ... If this life in the Nevada State Prison is an existence preparatory to the great hereafter, all I can say is that I pity the next one.

Hoping to hear from you soon ... I am your friend.
CHARLES JONES.

Jones had friends petitioning for his release, although it isn't clear how long that effort had been under way and for what reason. Jones had probably convinced them that the killing that got him sent to prison was in self-defense. He had likely contacted the prison reform association himself, hoping to get assistance in obtaining a new trial. He had good reason by today's standards, given that the judge who presided over his trial had watched the killing and yet testified as a witness.

Jones's second letter was dated June 28, 1871, two and a half months before the prison break. It reads in part:

> Mrs. L. H.: Dear friend—Your letter of June 23d was handed to me last night, and I am not capable of expressing my thanks to you for the pleasure of seeing those familiar faces that shine in freedom's light, but I am an exile, banished from a world of what once was happiness, but now is eternal punishment. My friend, you cannot imagine my feelings, at times, when I think of the past, my heart raises and chokes me. You say in your last letter that I have become reconciled to my fate, but that is a sad mistake; such can never be the case with me.

> I know no more about [the petition] than you at present … I am completely discouraged. I have give up all hopes of ever getting out of this place … If I get out this summer, send me that horse and I will pay you for him and all your trouble when I can get around.
>
> Give my best wishes to all that may inquire about me. Respectfully yours, CHARLES JONES.

The words "if I get out this summer" suggest that plans for the prison escape may have been under way when the letter was written because Jones was not scheduled for parole that summer or any time soon. It also appears he may have discussed the plans ("send me that horse") with Mrs. Hutchison.

The letters paint an eloquent picture of the despondency and desperation of incarcerated men. Yet it seems at odds with the rest of Jones's nature—his uncontrollable temper and his lack of remorse when he killed. He may have been schizophrenic or a brilliant psychopath.

Jones was born in Ireland, and his family settled in Ohio. The *Daily State Register* of October 7, 1871, stated that he was twenty-two years old, served in the federal army in the Civil War, and came to Nevada in 1866. It's doubtful he was twenty-two in 1871 because he would have been just sixteen years old when the war ended; that was possible but unlikely. He was probably in his twenties at the end of the war, which would be consistent with his family having left Ireland in the 1840s in the midst of its potato famine.

He was five foot ten and weighed in at about 150 pounds. He had small ears, light brown hair, hazel eyes, a thin black beard, a scar on his right hand, and an India ink tattoo of a ship on his arm. The ship may have been a reminder of the one that carried his family from Ireland, or perhaps it was for him a symbol of freedom.

For two or three years prior to his imprisonment, Jones had worked as a cowboy and teamster in Esmeralda County, Nevada, and in Inyo and Mono Counties in California. Among other things, he drove supply wagons serving mines and was familiar with local roads.

In 1869, Jones and men named Clark and Matthews drove a team and some saddle horses from Inyo County to the mining town of Hamilton in White Pine County in eastern Nevada. After an afternoon of hard drinking, Clark and Matthews got into a fistfight. Jones intervened, but Matthews wouldn't stop trying to get at Clark and threatened to pistol-whip both Jones and Clark. When Matthews stepped forward holding a pistol by the barrel in a raised hand, Jones pulled a knife from his boot and lunged at the suddenly backpedaling man, stabbing him in the heart and killing him. The local judge witnessed the incident from the courthouse window.

Jones hurriedly gathered his possessions and rode off on a saddle horse. A year later the Esmeralda County sheriff heard Jones was working as a blacksmith in California's Central Valley. The sheriff obtained extradition papers, located and arrested Jones, and transported him five hundred miles back to Hamilton. There he was convicted of second-degree murder and sent up for ten years. That he was familiar with the Central Valley gives some credence to an otherwise fanciful story of his eventual fate discussed later in these pages.

According to testimony at a trial of some of the escapees, Jones was the man who shot and killed Matthew Pixley during the battle at the prison, and Leander Morton was his "most active assistant." Thus, by the time he led a group of escaped prisoners south toward Bishop Creek, Jones had killed two men, by happenstance named "Matthew" and "Matthews." When he escaped from prison, Jones had little to lose. He was a desperate man, and his desperation would lead to more deaths.

2
Crossing the Pine Nut Mountains

The Sierra Nevada forms the western side of the Great Basin, the latter so named by John C. Fremont because waters flowing into it have no exit. As clouds are blown in off the Pacific Ocean and sweep over the Sierras, much of the moisture they hold drops on those lofty mountains, leaving little for points east. Water sources were a central consideration to the planning of the convicts who would trek south toward Bishop Creek. There would be significant stretches where water was scarce.

Prison Hill is a mile east of the prison, and the Carson River runs behind it. After getting outside the prison walls, several men led by Jones headed for the river and followed it upstream for a couple of miles, crossing to the east somewhere below Mexican Dam. A caretaker told authorities that around nine o'clock in the evening, a man in convict garb entered his cabin and demanded that he dress a wound. While occupied with the prisoner, he saw convicts breaking off their shackles with his tools. The man with the superficial wound was Frank Clifford, who had led the mob that dropped from the ceiling into the warden's quarters.

There were ten convicts by the time they assembled below the dam as they had planned. Four were headed for mines in the Silver Peak area, over two hundred miles south in the southern portion of Esmeralda County. These four, the "Silver Peak Group," would travel with the others for a day or so. These were the train robbers John Chapman and E. B. Parsons, who were looking at another couple of decades in prison, joined by Frank Clifford and Reno murderer George Roth. Roth and Clifford had once lived in White Pine County, as had Charlie Jones.

Their destination, Silver Peak, is in barren mountains about twenty miles west of Goldfield, Nevada, and due east of Bishop, California. The town was established when rich ore was struck in 1863. During the 1860s and '70s, it was notorious as one of the most wide-open, lawless places in the West, which explains why prison escapees would head there.

Today, Silver Peak is approaching ghost town status. Its primary employer, the Chemetall Foote Corporation, the only lithium producer in the United States, extracts and processes lithium from the dry lake floor of nearby Clayton Valley. Lithium, the third element formed at the beginning of the universe, after hydrogen and helium, has a significant array of useful properties: it is used, for example, in disposable and rechargeable batteries, in lenses with various uses, in pharmaceutical prescriptions, and in space and underwater equipment. The old miners, some of them from the San Francisco Bay area, named two large rock outcroppings on the dry lake "Alcatraz" and "Angel Island."

The other six escapees were the "Jones Group." Among them was the kid J. B. Roberts, who was in prison for robbery. His father, Chat Roberts, had hosted the train robbers at his saloon and had been a witness for the prosecution at their trial.

John Burke was also a part of this group. Despite a credible claim of self-defense, he had been found guilty of manslaughter after a brawl in Esmeralda County and sentenced to eight years. He was a Texan, short and thin with legs scarred from work as a cowboy, miner, and teamster. He had a strong moral sense and often expressed remorse for his part in the killing for which he was imprisoned. He would come to rue the fact that he joined Charlie Jones.

Train robber Tilton Cockerill, serving twenty years, was another of the Jones Group of six. A miner from Illinois, he had pulled off an infamous robbery with Squiers and Jack Davis in Six-mile Canyon in 1861. He had become a friend of Burke while in prison and would follow him, owing to Burke's familiarity with the mines around Silver Peak.

The remaining two men in the Jones Group were Leander Morton, who had fired scores of rounds during the prison gun battle, and Moses Black, serving an eight-year term for larceny committed in Nye County. The two, both from Ohio, were a strange pair.

The diminutive Irishman Morton, thirty years old, was looking at another fifteen years before he would even have a parole hearing. An intelligent, charismatic man, he was mean as hell, but like a lot of bad actors, he had a soft streak as shown by his friendship with Black.

Black was one of the largest men in the prison at over six feet two inches and two hundred pounds, with blue eyes and a fair complexion. Prison records identified him by a burst vein that created a dark streak down his lower leg. Except when his lack of common sense got him into trouble—for instance joining in the prison escape after being incarcerated only five days and certain to be released in less than two years—he was a rather docile man, a follower. A comparison of Morton and Black with Lenny and

George of John Steinbeck's *Of Mice and Men* wouldn't be far off the mark, although Black was somewhat smarter and a good deal meaner than poor George.

The route the Jones Group would follow would take them by the booming mining camp of Aurora, the seat of Nevada's Esmeralda County. Jones and Burke were familiar with the route to Aurora and past there to their ultimate destination of Bishop Creek at the foot of the Sierras in California's Inyo County. They were also familiar with and wary of the habits of vigilantes in Aurora, who tokened few scofflaws. Their trek would be one of epic proportions if completed—two hundred miles through rugged mountains and barren, arid valleys. The roads and trails were rutted, eroded, and at times difficult to find and follow, and water was scarce.

The new moon was three nights before the prison escape, and the first-quarter phase wouldn't be for another four, so the nights would be star speckled and pitch black. It was clear and cold and the men were without warm clothing. Their only food would be what they could find, steal, or shoot. Unless they could rustle horses, there was no chance of eluding capture.

Ten men walking in shackles left an easy trail for a posse. It was the two-hour jump on the pursuers after the escape, luck in quickly finding tools to get rid of the shackles, and the cover of darkness that got them through the night.

They made good time. After crossing the Carson River, they continued south on a worn wagon road toward Painted Rock, a familiar landmark. They were headed for Sunrise Pass Road at a point somewhere east of Painted Rock near Pipe Springs. The road connected the agricultural areas of the Carson Valley, which lies just east of the Sierras (and Lake Tahoe), with ranches in Smith and Mason Valleys on the other (eastern) side of the nearly ten thousand foot Pine Nut range. Their rapid progress on a black night suggests they had lanterns taken from prison stores. On the other hand, as many mountain travelers have found, starlight can often be enough to light a walker's way on black nights.

As they gained elevation, they could see lights from the hearths in ranch houses tucked up against the Sierras. Gas lanterns glowed at Genoa, the first settlement in Nevada, established by Mormon traders in 1851. They made out lights farther south at the way stations at Mottsville and Fairview and at Fredericksburg across the state line in California. The stations were along the road to Hangtown and the placer diggings in California's Western Sierra foothills.

They had walked south nearly twelve miles and it was after midnight when they reached Sunrise Pass Road. The road doubled back to the northeast and dropped down to Smith Valley. This was the route the men of the Silver Peak Group would follow. They parted with the Jones Group at Pipe Springs, the latter intending to head directly south.

On reaching Smith Valley in the early morning hours, the Silver Springs Group veered off to the southeast and struck the West Walker River near a popular hot springs. After following the river to a point where it joined the East Walker, they followed a well-traveled road east around the north end of the Wassuk Range. After a few miles, they met the main road that would take them on south to Silver Peak.[1]

They had traveled on foot over 75 miles in two days and were still faced with a trek through the desert of yet another 150 miles. As they rested by a campfire eating roasted coyote, they were surprised and captured by heavily armed riders who appeared out of the darkness. Train robbers Chapman and Parsons, along with fellow escapees Clifford and Roth, were returned to prison and the rewards collected. Clifford told authorities that if Warden Denver and trustee Bob Deadman had not been disabled so quickly, the escape would have failed at the start.

From Pipe Springs, the Jones Group headed south along a mining road that connected with Stockyard Road near Buckeye Spring. The latter road took them into Pine Nut Valley at a point west of the crest of the Pine Nut range and east of the Douglas County towns of Minden and Gardnerville. On reaching the valley, they spotted several cabins and horses. As they crept close in the shadows cast by the eastern ridges at dawn, they came upon a man identified

---
[1] Today's US Highway 95.

in newspaper accounts as "the Dutchman." They were able to surprise, overcome, and tie him to a wagon wheel.

The Dutchman was a "coal burner," a common occupation in mining country. Prospectors and miners had combed the range since the 1850s; there were several mines and a small mining town called Bullionville at the south end of the valley. Simple smelters were often constructed downslope from mines, and charcoal was a principal ingredient in the smelting process. A coal burner chopped and collected wood or sage or anything that could be "charcoalized" by being burned in pits. When it reached the right consistency after burning, it would be transported to the smelters. It took thirty to sixty bushels of charcoal to smelt a ton of ore.

The use of charcoal in mining operations dates to ancient Greece. The wood was commonly burned in pits, as was the case with the Dutchman. Italians, however, perfected the use of charcoal ovens. Made of stone, the ovens were tall beehive-shaped stone structures that made use of air currents for efficient burning at high temperatures. In 1876 Italian masons known as "carbonari" built the Ward charcoal ovens near Ely in eastern Nevada; they are preserved as examples of the craft.

The convicts saddled and rode off on the Dutchman's four horses. When a posse arrived six hours later, he was cussing a blue streak, infuriated at the theft of the work horses and tack essential to his occupation. A ride was located, and he joined the chase. He was lucky to be alive. According to a statement given later by escapee J. B. Roberts, convict Morton told the others that the Dutchman was the last man he would ever leave tied up. He said, ominously, "I once got nineteen buckshot in my backside by tying a man up instead of killing him. From now on I'll damn well kill all the rest."

The Dutchman told the posse there were six convicts, one of whom he heard the others call "Burke." They had three Henry rifles, a double-barreled shotgun, and one or two six-shooters that he could see. Hearing of the Henry rifles, the posse knew the convicts had superior firepower, so the decision was to keep the pressure on by continuing the chase but to avoid direct contact. The Henrys were mentioned days later in an article in Carson's *Daily State Register*.

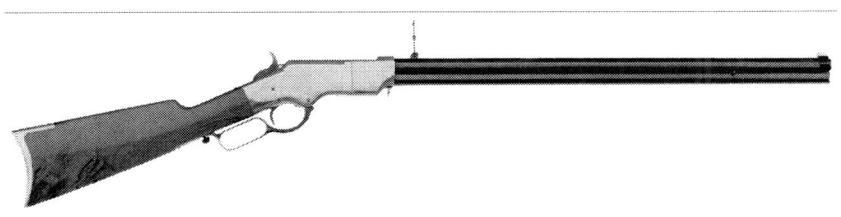

B. Tyler Henry invented his rifle just prior to the Civil War at the request of arms maker Oliver H. Winchester.

The Henry rifle was the deadliest personal weapon of its day. Arms maker Oliver H. Winchester hired gun designer B. Tyler Henry to make a reliable repeating rifle to replace the common single-shot muzzle loader used in the military and by frontiersmen. Henry first produced a metallic-cased cartridge, and then he turned to fashion the rifle that would use it. He designed a .44-caliber rimfire, lever-action rifle capable of rapid, accurate fire. He was granted a patent in 1860. Three of the earliest of the rifles—richly engraved, inscribed, and fitted with rosewood stocks—were presented to President Lincoln and the secretaries of war and the navy.

The Henry gave one man more firepower than a dozen marksmen with muskets. A rifleman could get off fifteen rounds in ten or twelve seconds. Although it was never officially adopted by the Union army during the Civil War, the Henry was used by some units and by individual troopers who could afford to purchase the rifle. It provided a huge edge in infantry combat and cavalry skirmishes. After an encounter with the Henry-armed Seventh Illinois Volunteer Infantry, a Confederate general remarked that it was "a rifle the Northerners could load on Sunday and fire all week."

The Henry evolved into the Winchester lever-action rifle seen in Western movies;[2] it is still produced. The Henry/Winchester is often cited as one of the three inventions that were most instrumental in the settling of the American West. The others were

---

[2] John Wayne pointedly slams his Henry on the desk as he registers at a little hotel in Durango, Mexico, in the 1971 oater called *Big Jake*. He has just seen the bad guys waiting outside.

Joseph Glidden's barbed wire fence and Daniel Halladay's windmill. Glidden, a farmer, patented barbed wire in 1874 and set up his Barb Fence Company in DeKalb, Illinois. He first manufactured the barbs with a common coffee mill. Halladay, a Connecticut machinist, designed this country's first commercially successful windmill. He was granted a patent in 1854 for a self-governing design that allowed the windmill to automatically turn to face changing winds and to control its speed of operation.

Riding the Dutchman's horses, the Jones Group continued south through Pine Nut Valley, passing east of Mount Siegel (9451') and several early mining sites before descending east through Red Canyon into Smith Valley. The upper reaches of the canyon are lush with meadows and a year-round creek, but it narrows as it emerges into the valley. Near the mouth exposed, reddish-tinted earth in the steep walls gives the canyon its name.

With four horses for six of them, the men took turns riding tandem or walking. The horses were startled from time to time as sage grouse took flight with a roar of wings customary of the species, but progress was continuous and without incident. That they encountered no one after running into the Dutchman proved the wisdom of choosing a route less traveled than the road over Sunrise Pass. As they emerged into the foothills above Smith Valley seven miles north of Wellington, they veered south again, staying among pines and cedars at the base of the mountains. The mining camp of Aurora was in the range fifteen or so miles directly behind Bald Mountain, which they could see twenty miles off to the south. Once beyond Aurora, Burke and Jones told them, they would be safe.

There was a general feeling of relief as the men road through the valley. They had just put a rugged mountain range between themselves and any pursuers who might be on their trail. The going would be easier for the next leg of their journey, at least in terms of terrain.

They struck the West Walker River near Wellington Station, a stop for supply wagons on roads converging from several directions. The supplies were headed for mines in Aurora, Silver Peak, and areas between. Wellington was a "way station," the functional equivalent of today's truck stop. Located along main wagon roads near water sources, usually around a half-day's or a day's ride apart, the stations provided food, lodging, and stable services, and they usually had a good stock of whiskey. Wellington Station was built in the 1850s. It was purchased by Daniel Wellington from Jack Wright and Len Hamilton in 1863. Jack Wright Pass is west of the tiny hamlet of Wellington on what was once the Esmeralda Road and is now Nevada State Route 208.

The road the convicts would follow south from Wellington to Aurora was a portion of the Esmeralda Road that had linked Aurora and Carson City since at least the early 1860s. For the next twenty-seven miles, the road followed a section of an Indian trail that John C. Fremont, Kit Carson, and their men had traversed during Fremont's expedition of 1843–44.

By the time the convicts hit the Esmeralda Road, it was thirty-six hours since the escape. They had traveled about forty-five miles, more than a third of the distance on foot. They would forge on past Wellington without rest to avoid detection. With barely a fourth of their journey behind, theirs was already a remarkable trek that would be difficult today for all but the fittest.

The men averaged five feet seven in height and about 140 pounds. The weight was quite a bit lower than today's average. This was in the days before refined sugar and white flour, the culprits in today's obesity epidemic. Meat was from range-fed or wild animals. There was little obesity except among the wealthy social classes. Heart disease was virtually unknown among working-class people. These men were miners, teamsters, or cowhands used to hard work and long hours, and they had just been at hard labor in prison.

They were in excellent physical condition. They needed to be in order to do what they had just done and to endure the rigors that lay ahead.

Compounding the physical difficulties were existential psychological factors. They were on the run; they knew they would be hotly pursued; they could be seen and shot at any time. They had been without sleep for a day and a half and were at times cold and always hungry. They faced extended sentences and horrible working conditions on the rock pile should they be returned to prison. Worse yet, the prison break had resulted in at least two deaths, so there could be a murder trial in the near future or an even more imminent lynch-party. They were all familiar with the doings of vigilantes.

They were near their breaking points. It would not be unlikely for any one of them to kill to remain free.

In *A Walk in the Woods*, his humorous story of his hike along parts of the Appalachian Trail, Bill Bryson, a comparative babe in the woods, was astounded when he began the hike through the thick woods at the start of the trail in northern Georgia. "Woods are not like other spaces," he says. "To begin with they are cubic. They make you feel small and confused and vulnerable; they are a vast and featureless nowhere." In short, he says, "Woods are spooky."[3]

After passing Wellington Station, the convicts would have to ride miles across wide-open, treeless plains and rolling sagebrush hills where a man on a horse could be spotted from miles away. In contrast to Bryson's "cubic" spaces, these could be called "planar" spaces. But just as in the case of Bryson's spaces, with a posse of heavily armed riders somewhere behind, "you sense an atmosphere of pregnant doom with every step [that] leaves you profoundly aware that you are out of your element and ought to keep your ears pricked."[4] To the convicts, these vast, featureless open spaces were as spooky as Bryson's woods.

3
Aurora and the Demise of the Daly Gang

Once on the Esmeralda Road, the Jones Group was on a heading for the mining town of Aurora, forty-seven miles distant. The town was in the Bodie Hills, eight miles east of what soon would become the Bodie town site. Like Virginia City, Aurora was one of the West's more prosperous—and notorious—mining towns.

In 1860, three tired prospectors from California discovered gold in a waterless gulch quite by accident and staked a claim. In deciding on a name for the mining district they intended to form, which

---

[3] Bryson, *A Walk in the Woods*, p. 44.
[4] Ibid.

would eventually include the Aurora town site, one of them suggested "Esmeralda." He had remembered the name of the young gypsy heroine of Victor Hugo's *The Hunchback of Notre Dame*, the tragedy in which a protagonist is the hunchback Quasimodo. The novel, published in 1831, was widely read in America.

In 1861, the Nevada Territorial Legislature divided the territory of over a hundred thousand square miles into nine counties, one of which was named after the mining district. When it became clear that the territory would be admitted to the Union, "Esmeralda" was a rival of "Nevada" for the state's name.[5]

Mining districts in the area eventually produced bullion that would be worth, today, nearly $400 million. It was a princely sum for a relatively short-lived boom, but it paled in comparison to the Comstock.

Until the state boundary was accurately surveyed, Aurora served as the county seat of both California's Mono County and Nevada's Esmeralda County. One Auroran was the Speaker of the California legislature at the same time as another was president of the Nevada Territorial Legislature. When a survey completed in 1864 placed Aurora in Nevada, the seat of Mono County was relocated to nearby Bridgeport.

Aurora may have been named after the goddess of the dawn of Roman mythology, although the origin of the name is uncertain. It's also possible someone made the obvious connection with the chemical symbol for gold: Au. ("Aurum" is Latin for gold.)

In 1861, Samuel Clemens traveled west with his older brother Orion, who had been appointed by Abraham Lincoln to serve as Nevada's territorial secretary. Curiosity took Sam from Carson City to Aurora, where he lived and did some prospecting and exploring in the early 1860s. In his book of reminiscences, *Roughing It*, published in 1872, he used the generic term "Esmeralda" to include Aurora and the surrounding areas, as did most of the citizenry.

When Clemens (he was not yet Mark Twain) lived in Aurora, it had "a population of two thousand people, twenty-two saloons, sixteen ore

---

[5] Nevada now has seventeen counties, including a large area surrounding Las Vegas that was split off by the legislature from Lincoln County in 1909 to form Clark County. Esmeralda County was also eventually split; its northern portion, which includes the Aurora ghost town, is now Mineral County.

mills, ten restaurants, two churches, one newspaper, a Masonic hall, an Odd Fellows hall, and an unspecified number of whorehouses."[6] The town reached its peak population of about 4,500 in 1865.

Later to become the country's most famous writer and lecturer under his pen name, the young Clemens honed his skills by writing pieces for Aurora and other newspapers. As a prospector, however, he had the luck of most of them—that is to say, none whatsoever.

As he contemplated what to do after realizing mining was not in his blood, the *Daily Territorial Enterprise* of Virginia City, one of the best-known newspapers in the West, hired Clemens as its city editor. He was amazed to be offered twenty-five dollars a week. "[I]t looked like a bloated luxury—a fortune, a sinful and lavish waste of money," he said.[7]

As a lark, Clemens had been writing letters from Aurora to the *Enterprise* under the pen name "Josh" in some of which he satirized Nevada chief justice George Turner. Turner's constant references to himself in speeches had induced Clemens to call him "Professor Personal Pronoun." The letters were popular and caught the attention of the editors.

When an opening arose on the newspaper's staff, the business manager of the *Enterprise*, who had known Orion and Sam Clemens when the three were involved with the territorial legislature, recommended that the editor hire Sam. In his position as territorial secretary, Orion controlled the valuable printing contract for the state's official documents, so the editor saw the light. It was a move that would assure the lasting fame of his newspaper.

William Wright, an author and writer for the *Enterprise*, became a close friend and roommate of Clemens. He had assumed the wonderful pen name Dan De Quille. Clemens liked it so much that he took a pen name himself and became, forevermore, Mark Twain, a term he'd used as a river boat pilot on the Mississippi. "Mark twain!" was the call for two fathoms, indicating a ship's passage from shallow to safe water. Historian Kevin Starr says, however, that despite his familiarity with the term on the river, when adopted by Clemens as a pen name "mark twain" was "either a riverboat term

---

[6] Morris Jr., pp. 89–90.
[7] Twain, p. 152.

or Virginia City saloon lingo for two free drinks, depending on which authority one is following."⁸ Twain's first known use of the name in writing is in his famous "Letter from Carson City" dated February 3, 1863.

De Quille had advised the pre-Twain Clemens, "Get the facts first, then you can distort them as much as you like." Twain put that advice to good use throughout his life.

Conditions on the Esmeralda were rough and accommodations primitive. The wooden cabin Clemens shared in Aurora was a one-roomer, maybe fifteen by twenty feet. It had a wood-burner stove; cardboard or tarpaper insulation provided a modicum of protection from winter's subzero temperatures.

Twain said there were two seasons in those mountains, the breaking up of one winter and the beginning of the next. It was so cold that "when a man calls for a brandy toddy there, the bar keeper chops it off with a hatchet and wraps it up in paper like maple sugar. And it is further reported that the old soakers haven't any teeth—wore them out eating gin cocktails and brandy punches."⁹

On taking his new employment in Virginia City after leaving the Esmeralda, Twain still dressed like a typical miner:

> I was a rusty-looking city editor, I am free to confess—coatless, slouch hat, blue woolen shirt, pantaloons stuffed into boot-tops, whiskered half down to the waist, the universal navy revolver slung to my belt. But I secured a more Christian costume and discarded the revolver. I had never had occasion to kill anybody, nor ever felt a desire to do so, but had worn the thing in deference to popular sentiment, and in order that I might not, by its absence, be offensively conspicuous, and a subject of remark. But the other editors, and all the printers ... carried revolvers.¹⁰

---

⁸ Starr, p. 139. Clemens had often experimented with pen names, including Sergeant Fathom, John Snooks, Thomas Jefferson Snodgrass, and W. Epaminondas Adrastus Perkins.
⁹ Twain, pp. 137–8.
¹⁰ Id. at p. 153.

Aurora, Nevada, about the time Mark Twain lived there. (Courtesy of Nevada Historical Society)

A superintendent and miners at the Ophir Mine in Virginia City, c. 1872. In 'Roughing It', Mark Twain described the clothing worn by miners and, indeed, the clothing he wore himself. He dressed pretty much like the man second from the right. (Courtesy of Nevada Historical Society)

(Courtesy of Nevada Historical Society)

The needs of Nevada miners gave rise to perhaps the most successful clothing venture in history. Jacob Youphes arrived in the United States from Riga, Latvia, in 1854. After working as a tailor in various places in the United States and Canada, and having changed his last name to Davis, he opened a shop in Virginia City in its boom days. In response to a woman's complaint that the seat of her miner husband's pants kept wearing out too quickly, he hit on the idea of affixing reinforced pockets to denim pants with copper rivets.

Davis purchased the denim cloth from one Levi Strauss of San Francisco. The pants were such a big seller that Davis and Strauss jointly applied to patent the process; the patent was granted in 1873. Davis eventually sold his interest to Strauss, worked as a superintendent of the clothing company, and retired a happy, wealthy man. The rest, as they say, is history.

Full beards were the norm on the frontier, as were pipes, cigars, and hand-rolled cigarettes. Twain himself was a lifelong pipe smoker. Pistols and knives were commonly carried and often used in barroom confrontations. Single-shot derringers were often hidden somewhere on the person.

No one went thirsty in Aurora for lack of watering holes, and there were as many gambling houses and brothels as saloons. Francis P. Farquhar observed, "[H]ere ... where men are congregated and living uncomfortably, where there are no home ties or social checks, no churches, no religions—here one sees gambling and vice in all its horrible realities. Here, too, are women—for nowhere else does one see prostitutes as he sees them in a mining town."[11] That description also fit Virginia City.

For the most part, the miners lived payday to payday. After grabbing the paycheck and stocking up on supplies for the week, it was off to the saloons and gambling houses; what money wasn't drunk up or gambled away would likely be spent in a hurdy-gurdy down the canyon. (A hurdy-gurdy was a musical instrument, an organ of sorts, commonly found in Western bars, that was played by turning a crank. For reasons unique to the time and place, the term also referred to a bordello.)

Violence and lawlessness were part of life in mining towns. Shootings and shoot-outs among toughs and goons hired to protect the mines were regular events. The fighting was usually a product of drink. Apart from beer and whiskey, most of it made in unknown distilleries, there were concoctions such as Pisco punch, a strong mix of largely unknown content and alcohol proportion that varied according to the whims of the bartender. Another favorite was the forty-rod, a raw brand of whiskey that derived its name from the distance an inexperienced imbiber could walk before collapsing.

A little town called Lee Vining sits at the foot of the Sierras alongside Mono Lake, near the turnoff to the eastern entrance to Yosemite National Park. It bears the name a man from Indiana of Quaker descent who came west to seek his fortune. In 1857 he built a sawmill on a nearby creek that also bears his name. He began selling lumber on the Esmeralda in 1861.

The stories of his untimely death vary in detail. One story, the most likely, is that he was in Aurora in the Exchange Saloon when a gun battle erupted. When order was restored, he was lying dead on the wooden sidewalk. A shot to the groin had severed a femoral artery. The coroner found that a derringer in his pocket had inflicted the fatal wound. He had accidentally pulled the trigger as he reached for the little pistol to defend himself.

---

[11] Farquhar, *Up and Down California*, p. 420.

Another version has him in a saloon drinking up the profits of a lumber sale when he fingered the derringer as he reached to scratch his groin. The explosion cleared the saloon. He was found facedown on a road out of town, having slowly bled to death.

Aurorans made use of the "citizens' safety committee," a euphemism for vigilantes bent on doing justice by their own standards when they felt the law wouldn't exert sufficient punishment on a wrongdoer. "Justice" occasionally meant banishment, but in a good many cases it took the form of a hangman's knot.[12]

Convicts Burke and Jones, who had often driven team through Aurora in the 1860s, were aware of the case of the notorious Daly Gang. John Daly's fate was their on minds as the escapees began the ride from Wellington toward Aurora.

James Sears stole a horse from a guest at a way station on the banks of the West Walker and headed for Aurora on the Esmeralda Road. Station keeper William Johnson ordered a hired hand, John Rogers, to chase the thief and return the horse.

After twenty miles hard riding, Rogers caught up with Sears in Sweetwater Valley. When Sears refused to dismount and made threats, Rogers drew his Colt navy revolver and fatally shot Sears. He delivered the body to authorities in Carson City the next day. Based in part on evidence that Sears was a member of the notorious Daly Gang, a coroner's jury found that the killing was justified.

John Daly, at age twenty-five, was one of the West's most feared outlaws. A New Yorker of Irish parentage, he had earned a reputation as a gunfighter in Sacramento and Virginia City and as far north as the Fraser River country in western Canada. His fearful reputation was built on stories that he had killed eleven men.

Daly and his boys arrived in Aurora in early 1863. According to a post by the Mineral County Museum, they had been hired to provide security for the Pond Mining Company. The Pond was fighting the Real Del Monte Mining Company over claims to Last Chance Hill. The companies hired gunmen to intimidate one another and to keep witnesses out of court. The feud accounted for

---

[12] The last old-fashioned Western-style lynching in California—of five men in Modoc County—took place in May, 1901. (Starr, p. 85.)

the bulk of the violent deaths of twenty-seven men in one year in and around Aurora.

The newspapers called Daly's modus operandi "criminal vigilantism." Anyone who resisted the demands of Daly's employer of the moment would be taken and lynched. As hired guns, the Daly bunch terrorized the Nevada gold fields for two years.

At one time they virtually ran Aurora. By way of fraud and threat, they garnered enough votes to have one of their number elected marshal. The horrified editor of the *Esmeralda Star* wrote, "No sooner had the marshal been sworn in than the worst villains that ever infested a civilized community were appointed policemen, and with but few exceptions they were composed of as hard a set of criminals that ever went unhung."

Not long after John Rogers killed gang member Sears, Daly showed up at William Johnson's way station and asked where he might find Mr. Rogers. When Johnson refused to tell him, Daly stormed off, resolved that both Rogers and Johnson would die.

On a morning in the winter of 1864, Johnson rode along the Esmeralda Road up to Aurora to peddle potatoes he had kept in his cellar. Afterward, he wandered to a saloon where he was befriended by a man who, unknown to him, was a Daly crony. As Johnson emerged from another saloon dead drunk at four in the morning, Daly and gang member William Buckley were waiting. Two other Daly confederates, James "Massey" Masterson and John McDowell, alias "Three-Fingered Jack," were lingering nearby engaged in drunken banter. Buckley felled Johnson with the butt of a pistol, and Daly shot him in the head. Buckley severed Johnson's jugular vein with a bowie knife, his blood staining the board sidewalk. Daly had avenged his crony, the late James Sears.

By midmorning, the grisly murder was the talk of the town; the people were furious. A coroner's inquest was launched, and by evening, hundreds of men had formed the "Aurora citizens' safety committee." John A. Palmer was named first officer. In 1858, he had performed similar services in Tuolumne County on the western side of the Sierras. He was, in effect, the chief executioner.

The coroner located a percipient witness who testified as the inquest continued later in the week. He gave the sordid details of the murder. Others witnesses described Daly's crude and threatening actions leading to the crime, some testifying that they had often heard him say he would kill William Johnson on the spot should he see him. Several witnesses testified in secret because Daly had put word on the street that anyone giving evidence against him would die.

Based on the findings of the inquest, the court issued warrants, and Daly, Three-Fingers, and Massey were arrested in town and jailed. The citizens' committee declared martial law. The members of the Daly Gang who were not involved in Johnson's murder were ordered to leave town, which they did post haste.

After a search in Adobe Meadows and around Mono Lake, William Buckley was captured near Rush Creek in the Mono Basin. He had eluded capture for four days in an extreme Mono winter, having walked nearly a hundred miles without food and with clothing that did little to protect him in the subfreezing temperatures. He told his captors he would rather be hung than suffer such miseries again.

The coroner's jury, without taking any exculpatory testimony, found that Daly, Three-Fingers, Massey, and Buckley had murdered William Johnson with malice aforethought. As preparations for a trial that would never happen were underway, members of the citizens' committee took possession of the jail. Hours later, the committee convened and in short order condemned the men.

Businesses in the area were ordered closed, including the outlying mines and mills. Carpenters constructed a gallows in the center of Silver Street near the bluff north of Pine Street. The next morning thousands gathered with holiday exuberance.

The telegraphed warning of Nevada governor James Nye that there should be no violence was ignored. At noon a citizens' guard marched Daly and his boys to the hanging ground to a slow-cadenced drumbeat. With fixed bayonets the guards formed a square around the gallows and stood at attention as the doomed men climbed the thirteen steps to the platform. It was said that they walked "with a firm step" and when on the platform they "surveyed the crowd with apparent cool indifference."[13]

---

[13] See McGrath, p. 95, et. seq. The quotes depicting the death of Daly and his boys are taken in part from Professor McGrath's description of their lynching, which is based on articles in Aurora newspapers. His painstakingly researched and well-written book is a classic study of violence in the Old West, although its scope is much broader.

John Daly took a drink of brandy handed up from the crowd and pointed at a member of the citizens' committee who was holding a pistol. "You son of a bitch. If I had a six-shooter I would make you get."

He took several silver dollars out of his pocket and threw them into the crowd. Shouting down at the assembled masses, he called William Johnson, his victim, a "damn old Mormon thief … had I lived I would have wiped out Johnson's whole generation." He said that he and Buckley were the killers and that Three-Fingered Jack and Massey were innocent men.

"That's right," Buckley said, pointing. "They're innocent." He beckoned a friend to the foot of the platform and asked him to pay his just debts. Then, looking out at the crowd, he said, "Adieu, boys. I wish you all well. All of you boys must come up to my wake in John Daly's cabin tonight. Be sure of this. Goodbye. God bless you all."

He stepped aside and dictated a letter in which he asked a friend to "give my first and last love to my dear, dear mother" but "don't let her know that my death was the ignominious death of the gallows … Pray for me, for I have yet hopes in a merciful God and Savior."

Three-Fingered Jack yelled out, "I am as innocent of this as the child unborn. This is murder! You are going to murder me, gentlemen." Friends approached the platform, and he knelt and reached to them. When he stood up he brandished a derringer and tried to kill himself with a shot to the chest, but the pistol misfired. He threw it to the ground. "That son of a bitch of a pistol has fooled me!" Realizing the futility of the situation, his last words were "I'll die like a tiger."

James Masterson was next. He said simply, with both hands stretched out, palms up, "Gentlemen, I am innocent."

The pleas fell on deaf ears. The crowd surged forward, demanding justice. A voice cried out to get on with it and cheers erupted. A dirge-like thump of the drums began; guards tied and blindfolded the four men, and nooses were positioned to make sure the hangman's knot would efficiently serve its purpose.

Quiet came over the crowd as the good Reverend Yeager offered a prayer. The drums surged to a loud roll, cannons roared, and the trap door dropped. In seconds the town was free of festering evil. The saloons and hurdy-gurdies had swell turnouts that night.

That was the Aurora toward which the Jones Group was riding. They'd have been well advised to tread lightly. They did not.

4
The Mail Rider Billy Poor

Cockerill calls out, "Jones, goddamn it, you got us through those mountains. We're gonna do it, we're gonna make Bishop Creek!"

Jones jerks the reins and looks back. "Wasn't just me. We got to send a note to the old coal burner and thank him for the loan of his horses."

The kid Roberts riding alongside Jones laughs and reaches over and slaps him on the shoulder.

They're past Wellington Station headed south. The next stretch will take them eight miles over rolling, sage-covered hills on a heading for the narrows of Dalzell Canyon and eventually Sweetwater Summit. The horses pick up the pace as they smell the water in the meadows beyond the mouth of the canyon. Bald Mountain looms ever closer as the light of the waning afternoon climbs toward its top. From a hill near the canyon they wheel and look back at the peaks of the Pine Nut Range, bathed in evening purple. They can see for miles with not a soul in sight. They heave collective sighs and spirits rise.

Burke pulls the group together and points at the canyon. "We go through there a couple miles. We'll see where it gets real narrow, just wide enough for a stage alongside the gully. Just before that there's a road into the hills off to the west where there's a spring." He points toward the ridges right of the canyon. "We post a watch up there." He pats his horse on the neck. "These horses need rest. We make camp and build a fire down low by the spring where it won't be seen."

"We need to eat. I suppose we could shoot a deer, but shots would be heard," Morton says. "Maybe there's some ripe pine nuts. I could use something in my gut."

"Amen," Roberts says.

As they reach the spring, Burke says "I'll post watch on the ridge."

They build a campfire in a glade among man-high rocks where the light will be shielded. There's little talk as they stare at the fire and doze off one by one.

In the early morning hours, Morton douses the fire. It's cold and so dark that starlight paints the ground with shadows of the surrounding pines. The lonely howls of coyotes are all that break the silence.

Sitting on a bluff above the camp, Burke is sure that anyone trailing them has stopped for the night in Wellington. It's so quiet that he figures any sound will ride the breeze for miles and wake him. Despite being bone tired, he doesn't sleep right away.

What if I leave now and post down by the road and wait for the posse to get me? He knows most men get paroled well short of their full sentences; at most he'll serve maybe a couple more years. But maybe it won't be so easy if a posse spots him. That happens and he might get shotgunned.

He lodges himself into a crevasse in the rocky bluff to avoid the cold wind and pulls up a saddle blanket and drifts off.

He wakens at first light. It's dead quiet as he stretches his cold limbs. He looks back over the broad rolling plain toward Wellington and watches the gray morning take on color as the sun climbs behind the eastern ridges. The ravens and nutcrackers, usually the roustabouts of the morning, are strangely silent. *Some kind of omen?*

He hikes back down the hill and finds Jones and Morton stirring the fire, keeping it burning hot to keep the smoke down. He sits on a rock. "We got to figure out what goes from here on out."

"The horses need more rest, and so do we. Hell, I'm flagged. This is a good spot to sit a bit," Jones says. "What say, Burke?"

Burke nods. "I could see miles. We keep someone posted up there and wait and leave here midmorning."

"Yeah," Morton says. "If they come this way, we're far enough off the trail they'll ride right by."

Burke bends down and draws in the dirt with a stick. Roberts and Cockerill are at the fire now. Burke yells for Black to join them.

"This here's how the meadows are laid out in the canyon up there a piece. There's cows all along and a barn and a house where the dairyman and his family stay. It's up there maybe two miles, past some sulfur springs. We need to send somebody to scout it, see if there's anyone around, anything to eat."

"Roberts is our man," Jones says.

Burke points at Roberts. "We got a job for you." He turns back to working the dirt. "The road goes over the summit, and we're down to Sweetwater before we know it. There's plenty of water and grass along the way. We take our time, keep in the trees along the meadows. Stop a lot to let the horses feed."

"Jesus, why take our time? Why wait?" Black asks.

Burke points at Jones. "Jones will tell you we don't want to be anywhere near Aurora in the daylight. They'll spot us for sure, and there's some ornery folks live there. I'm sure they've been telegraphed with word of us breaking out."

"They got a safety committee that'll string us up on the spot," Jones says. "Just like they did with old John Daly and his boys."

"Sure'n hell," Burke says.

Burke bends over his map again. "It's about ten miles to Sweetwater. We want to get there late afternoon. Then it's three miles to the Walker River and another five miles downriver to the station at the Elbow. We get past there just before dark, leave the river, and make our way up toward the Esmeralda, straight south into the mountains."

"We stay clear of Aurora?" Cockerill asks.

"Absolutely," Burke says. "When it gets dark, we hole up a few miles east of town, and at first light we hit the road down to Alkalai Valley and Mono. That's California; we should get down there by midmorning."

Jones chimes in. "Me and Burke know the way, and we can make time as long as we can see anything. I'd like to ride all night, but it'll be too dark, and we could easy get off track."

He stands and loads his cheek with a plug taken from the coal burner. "Should hit Bishop Creek by Sunday or even quicker, boys. If we get separated, two of the people I know there are Cap Smith and Bill Gill. They'll take care of us." He spits and gives a thumb up. "Not long now."

"Hoo boy," Black says, smiling.

Burke looks at Roberts. "You might run into the dairy boy. Be careful; don't let him spot you and figure out what's going on when he sees those goddamn prison pants."

He points up the canyon. "Get on out of here now. We'll be up there in a couple hours. If we're not, just come on back."

Jones says, "I'd sure like to meet that damn Dingman coming down the road. He'd be a dead man."

"Who's Dingman?" Burke asks.

"He's a bastard from Aurora who rides mail along here. He killed two men when he was working guard in the prison." Jones lifts a clenched fist. "We swore to get the son of a bitch. Kill him."

"Don't do anything crazy, Jones," Burke says. "We just want to get away from whoever is out there looking for us. We don't need to do anything stupid to call attention to us. Forget it. Anybody passes by, just get the hell out of sight and let 'em go."

"Damn right," says Cockerill. "You'll get us hung. Kill him on your own time, but leave us out of it."

Roberts mounts, rides back down to the main road, and starts up the canyon. He passes hot springs steaming in cold morning air that hints of sulfur and watches for fresh tracks on the road. He flinches as noisy jays screech and dart in and out of the shadows of the piñons. Dairy cows graze in the narrow meadows along the brook snaking down the canyon.

He ties his horse in a draw off the road and walks warily toward a ramshackle house and barn sitting near a pond just off the road. He sees the dairyman walk into the trees a mile or so up the canyon. Seeing and hearing nothing nearby, he climbs through a slat fence made of tree limbs and thin wire and begins to dig carrots and potatoes out of a half-acre garden. There's a noise and dust kicks up where the road disappears around a tree-covered hillside jutting into the meadow. He scrambles for cover among cornstalks and waits. As a lone rider comes around the bend he lies prone, fingering his pistol.

The rider passes twenty yards away. A young man. *Hell, he's no older than me. Nothin' to be scared of there.* He sees by the marked saddlebags that it's a mail rider. *Probably on the Aurora-to-Wellington run.* If they're on the road by now, he hopes the convicts will see the rider coming and get back into the trees. *Not smart to fool with no mail rider.*

Ten minutes after the rider disappears down the canyon, Roberts mounts and follows, staying along the grassy banks of a creek to keep the dust down. He reins his horse in as the sound of a gunshot echoes up the canyon, followed quickly by another. *Oh no!* He cuts back to the road and kicks his horse as he heads in the direction of the mail rider and the gunshots.

After a half mile, he finds Burke, Cockerill, and Black on the road, stopped, looking back toward where they had left Jones and Morton.

Burke is furious. "I know goddamn well who fired those shots. That rider didn't see us, and he shouldn't have seen Morton and Jones if they'd just kept quiet. He'll be telling everyone in Wellington he heard gunshots."

Mounting up later than the others, Jones and Morton reach the main road and turn and ride back up the trail to where they had camped to make it look like they're still up there. They then ride back toward the main road on rocky areas in the sagebrush off the trail to hide their tracks. Just as they reach the road, they see the mail rider.

"Damn," says Morton. "I think the man seen us. Have to stop him, Jones. How can we let a man go who's seen us in these prison clothes? He'll be down at Wellington in no time. Then we're good as dead."

Jones nods and pulls his shirt to hide the pistol in his waistband.

"I'll pull a trigger with any man," Morton says.

"I'm your man," Jones replies.

The rider waves as he rides up to them. He reins back when he sees the prison stripes.

"Where you headed, son?" Jones says.

"Wellington. Name's Billy Poor. First day carrying mail from Aurora for Bill Wilson."

Morton reaches down and grabs the bridle of Poor's horse. "We need to get some directions. Mind if we ride up the trail a bit to the spring where we can get a drink and relax and talk? You can show us how to get to Aurora." He points at the trail back in the direction of the convicts' prior night's camp.

"Look, I don't mean you men no harm. Far as I care, I ain't never even seen you men," a startled Poor says.

Morton starts up the trail leading Poor's horse. As he looks back, Jones puts his forefinger to his temple like he's shooting himself. Morton gives a slight nod.

Two hundred yards up the trail, Jones says, "Billy, do you know a Captain Dingman?"

"Yes," Poor says. "He'll be coming down on the stage from Esmeralda tomorrow. How do you know him?"

"Doesn't matter," Jones says. "Let's just say his goose is cooked." He laughs.

Poor is looking for a chance to bolt and ignores Morton's order to get off his horse. Jones dismounts and walks over to pull him off.

As Poor struggles with Jones, Morton pulls a pistol from his waistband and shoots the mail rider point blank in the back of the head.

Poor topples face-first in the dirt. Jones leans over and gives him the coup de grâce, with the ball coming out an eye in a spray of blood. "Solves our problems, huh Morton?"

They drag Poor's body to where the campfire was that morning, the heels of his boots making furrows in the sandy trail. They take his clothes off and find his coat and extra clothes in his saddlebags, along with hardtack and a canteen.

Jones tries Poor's clothes on and likes the fit.

Morton stomps around in Poor's boots. "They don't fit too good, but they'll be easier walking. I'll give my prison boots to Cockerill."

As Morton relights the fire and gets it going with hot-burning mahogany branches, Jones dresses Poor's shoeless corpse in prison pants and shirt.

"Let's make damn sure they won't know him when they find him," Jones says.

They use rocks to crush Poor's face to unrecognizable pulp, put him face-first in the fire, and stoke it to red-hot. They pile more fuel on Poor's head and shoulders and leave.

"Anyone finds him will think he's one of us," Jones says.

"Maybe, maybe not. But what the hell do we care now?"

Morton rides Poor's fresh horse, and they head back to the Esmeralda Road leading the extra animal.

"Damn lucky we got his horse; damn lucky," Jones says.

"Speed us up good, and we sure'n hell won't have to worry about him turning us in." Morton lets out a cackling laugh.

"Who's that?" Burke says, pointing. They recognize Jones and Morton coming up the road and ride quickly toward them.

"Where'd you get the new pony and the civilian clothes?" Roberts asks.

"Oh, we made us a raise," Jones says, smiling. "Got ourselves lucky."

"You shot the mail rider! That was the shots. That's about the stupidest thing you could ever do. Now the whole country will be after us." Burke is loud, his face red and contorted.

"You can bet for goddamn sure he has family in Aurora. I'm taking this Henry, and me and Cockerill are getting the hell away from you fools." He holds the rifle in the air. "You're as good as dead, and I ain't dying with you." He jerks the reins, and his horse wheels to start up the road.

Morton moves to block Burke's way. "Go if you want, but you ain't taking no horse and no Henry."

"Try and stop me, and I'll shoot your guts all over the road." Burke lifts the rifle high, pointed heavenward, menacing, finger on the trigger.

Cockerill says, "Burke's right. You two got no more sense than a fool hen."

Jones butts in. "Okay, Burke. We only meant to keep the kid with us until we were sure nobody was coming after him or looking for him. But he threatened us, and we were sure he would rat on us soon as he got to Wellington. We had to stop him, like it or not. We were saving you as much as ourselves."

Burke rides close to Jones. He leans over and spits off to the side and says, "Bullshit. You're lying, and you know it. You shot the kid because you wanted his horse and gun. Twice you shot him. You wanted him dead. You could have just taken his horse and let him walk."

Burke jerks the reins so hard his horse rears. His voice is high and breaking. "Hell, we'd be long gone by the time he walked to Wellington and they rounded up a posse. I don't go a cent on no cold-blooded murder. I don't care what excuse you come up with, Jones."

Cockerill intervenes. "Burke, we best all stick together to Bishop Creek. There's more firepower with more of us, and they can't chase us all if we scatter. When we get there, Jones can see his friends, and you and me can just gear up and get ourselves the hell on over to Silver Peak."

Burke spits toward Morton and yells, "Fools!" He reins around and starts up the road. The rest follow, Jones and Morton in the rear. After they pass the dairy farm, Roberts yells to Burke to look back. Jones and Morton have stopped. Burke and Roberts ride back to them.

"Roberts, you said you spotted the dairy farmer when he was scouting up here this morning," Jones says. "He's probably here without family. We wouldn't kill no family, but me and Morton figure he might have spotted us, and he damn sure heard the shots."

"We have to find him and take care of him," Morton says. He reins to ride back toward the farm.

"Stop!" Burke is as furious as before, but his expression has become one of cool self-possession.

His strained neck muscles stand out, betraying his effort to hide his anger. He speaks slowly, deliberately, emphasizing each word. "You go back there, and I'll be gone. Killing the kid was coward enough, but," he points at Jones, "you kill that dairyman, and damned if I won't go to Esmeralda and turn state's evidence."

He points at Morton. "I'll lead the sheriff after you, and I'll testify to put you in the grave. I'll cheer when they lead you up the stairs to the noose like they did Daly and Three-Fingers."

Burke turns and starts to ride up the canyon. Cockerill comes from behind and rides alongside him. "They're following us. Your talk about turning state's evidence put the fear in 'em."

They ride south up and out of the canyon, cross a wide pass off the side of Bald Mountain, and descend onto a broad, sage-covered, rolling plain. The two-mile high Sweetwater Mountains loom a mile off to the west. Cattle and deer gaze in meadows created by the perpetual runoff.

Jones points out the Sierras thirty miles off to the south as the snowcapped peaks of the monster range begin to appear above the canyon carved out by the East Walker River. "That there's the peak above Lee Vining's old camp in the Mono Basin," he says pointing. "Bishop Creek's about seventy miles down range. We're closing in, boys; we're getting near."

After another mile, Burke motions Cockerill to stop. "See them twin peaks in the main range? The Dunderberg Mine is just to the north. Dog Creek flows off the mountains there, and the diggings at old Dog Town are just a few miles this way from the peaks. I knew men who placer mined there in the fifties."

"Why don't we head over that way and find work?" Cockerill asks. "Hell, its right there. Maybe twenty miles."

"We're too late," Burke says. "The mines are mostly dead, and there's nothing more to placer. There wasn't much gold. What they found was pretty good for a while, but it got picked over fast."

"Too bad," Cockerill says. "If there was anything worth the trouble over there, I'd sure and leave Jones in a minute."

"In a heartbeat," Burke says. "The son of a bitch."

Five miles past the summit they warily approach the way station at Sweetwater; sensing the tension, the horse Roberts is riding rears and snorts, nearly throwing him. Skirting the station they reach Sweetwater Creek where the road veers toward the East Walker River. Following the road abutting the meadows and creek two miles more, they reach the river and follow it past the station at the Elbow, where the river makes a horseshoe bend[14] before continuing its easterly flow to Walker Lake and the arid reaches of the Great Basin. They spook dogs but don't see anyone in the twilight. The lanterns at the station haven't been lit.

They ride the Esmeralda Road southeast away from the river into the mountains until they reach a spot below Ninemile Ranch[15] where the road crosses Rough Creek and splits. It's nearly dark as they break and make camp off in the pines and willows bordering the creek. Roberts posts the first watch.

---

[14] A horseshoe bend in a river is also called an "oxbow."
[15] Mark Twain mentions Ninemile Ranch in *Roughing It*.

Black and Morton move off by themselves to a place downstream hidden in the willows. After a wordless interval as they stretch out, Black says, "yeah," mostly to himself and then louder to Morton. "Yeah, Burke is right. Why'd you kill that mail rider, Morton? They'll string us all up. Even us who didn't do nothing." *Goddamn it, I'd have been out in a year.*

After a pause, he says quietly, "You know, Morton, I should've stayed back in prison and waited until they let me out."

"Come on," Morton says. "Just hang on. Ain't no time for wishing after something else. After we stock up in Bishop Creek, you and me can head out where no man can find us." He struggles to his feet and walks to the creek. "Won't be long now and you're gonna find yourself a new life, maybe over in California," he says over his shoulder.

Black picks a pine nut off the ground and cracks it. "You think so? You really think so?" He sits back against a log with his hands behind his head, feet outstretched. "God, I hope you're right, Morton."

Silence as the two men gaze at the last of the orange sunset, just a thin glow lining the crest of the Sweetwater range. Stars begin to puncture the sky, accentuating the early glow of Venus, and the canyon winds subside as the night's cool sets in.

"I sure don't want no lynch party," Black says. "I seen a man strung up, and it ain't no pretty sight. He was bawling like a sick calf before they sprung the trap, and I heard him just keep on bawling after he dropped."

He grows silent. "Maybe it was in a dream I thought I heard him after he dropped," he finally says quietly to the darkness.

Burke crosses a meadow and climbs a hill to where he can watch back down the Esmeralda Road in what's left of the light. He's there as much to get away from Jones as he is to keep watch. He falls into deep sleep until a deer startles him. As dark turns to faint gray, he rushes to wake the other men.

"Get yourselves up, and let's get going. They'll be out after us at first light."

Leading the Dutchman's horse he's been riding, he tugs on Morton's sleeve. "Me and Cockerill will meet you where the Alkali Road splits off from the road to Aurora. Jones knows where it is."

5
The Funeral

Billy Poor's decomposed body was found and taken to Aurora on October 4, 1871, a day less than two weeks after his death. His face had been burned beyond recognition. His body had been pecked at by ravens and his limbs partially consumed by coyotes. He was identified by his riding crop and glove, and through a painstaking postmortem examination. The autopsy report generated unspeakable horror among the people. The prison clothes he had been dressed in made it clear who had murdered him.

The funeral and burial were with Episcopal rites. Business houses closed; flags were at half-mast. A deep feeling of grief prevailed in the community for months.

The mood of the people was captured in an Aurora citizen's letter to a Reno newspaper published ten days after the funeral.

> For three or four weeks, scarcely anything has been talked or thought of in this community but the doings of the escaped ... convicts ... The killing, by this band, of Wm. A. Poor, the pony express rider, was one of the most brutal, inhuman murders ever perpetrated on the Pacific Coast. Not content with the simple murder of their defenseless victim, these fiends seemed to revel in the diabolical work, and perpetrated outrages upon the dead body of the innocent boy, the mere thought of which is to chill the blood in the veins of the most savage Apache in Arizona. The horrible and shocking details of the murder as appeared from the condition of the body and its surroundings, when found, is a secret in the breast of two or three men, and out of regard for the feelings of the bereaved family will not be divulged unless elicited in some law court on the trial of the surviving perpetrators of this cowardly deed.

CHAPTER 6

The Fatal Affair in Monte Diablo Canyon

1
The Devil Mountain

*I*t was the predawn of Wednesday, September 20, 1871, two and a half days after the prison escape. The convicts were nervous as they assembled where the road split. One fork headed off toward Aurora; the other they would follow fifteen miles south to the relative safety of Alkali Valley across the state line in California.

This would be the most dangerous part yet of their flight to Bishop Creek. The lynching of the Daly Gang in Aurora seven years earlier preyed on their minds. It was fair warning that Aurorans were not given to mercy. They knew that once mail rider Billy Poor's body was found, the noose was certain if they were captured anywhere near the town.

What they didn't know concerned them as well. They figured someone must be on their trail, yet despite constant watch, they had seen no sign of pursuers. Prison records showed that Jones and Burke were familiar with the territory; surely someone must have figured out where they were headed.

They would ride single file just far enough apart for a man to keep track of the rider ahead. At one point they would be no more than six miles from Aurora, and they would pass several working mines and ranches. Burke would ride lead and give a hand signal to get off the road should he spot anyone. The hope was to reach Alkalai Valley by around seven o'clock in the morning.

The men were lucky Poor hadn't been found. He had left the station at Sweetwater around one o'clock in the afternoon on Tuesday, so he was killed by Jones and Morton an hour or so later. He wasn't reported missing in Aurora until Wednesday afternoon, when it was learned he'd failed to reach Wellington. Bill Wilson, the owner of the mail service that employed Poor, looked for him that day by retracing his route along the Esmeralda Road and checking adjacent stock trails. On Thursday, the newspapers were reporting him missing.

The speculation in some quarters was that he'd met up with the convicts and that they had tied him up somewhere and taken his horse. Others assumed he'd been taken captive and was riding with the convicts as protection.

With the exception of the furious Dutchman, who would show up at Aurora alone, the posse trailing the men from Carson City had given up the chase. Word that they had pulled back was telegraphed from Wellington to Esmeralda County sheriff John Helm in Aurora.

A report also reached Helm that the convicts had been seen crossing the East Walker River near the Elbow late Tuesday. Yet another report that had them close by Aurora early Wednesday morning stated that Billy Poor was with riding them. Eyewitness reports are often wrong, and the latter was an example, both because the convicts were always miles from Aurora and because Poor wasn't with them. This report was the source of rumors that would persist for two weeks that Poor was alive. The word of these alleged sightings reached Helm at about the time late Wednesday afternoon that Bill Wilson returned to say that his search had not turned up any sign of Poor.

Helm commissioned a posse headed by deputy sheriff John A. Palmer, the man who had supervised the lynching of the Daly Gang eight years earlier. It included Billy Poor's brother Horace and several deputies and citizens, some of whom had also witnessed Daly's death. The chase didn't begin until Wednesday evening, giving the convicts nearly a full day's head start.

After passing Spring Peak well before sunup Wednesday, the convicts met the Aurora and Owens River Wagon Road as it angled in from Aurora. Plans for the road were approved by commissioners appointed by the Mono County Board of Supervisors in 1862, when Aurora was still considered the seat of that county as well as the seat of Nevada's Esmeralda County. The Nevada Territorial Legislature authorized construction of the road in 1864, the statute being registered with and signed by territorial secretary Orion Clemens. It would link Esmeralda and environs with the economies of California's Owens Valley.

In their teamster days Jones and Burke had driven the length of the road. The comparatively easy travel it afforded figured prominently in Jones's thinking in planning his escape route and in convincing the other men how quickly they would reach Bishop Creek once they passed Aurora.

Passing through the open spaces of Alkali Valley in the early daylight hours, the convicts crossed the pole-line road connecting Lee Vining with Aurora just about where it crossed the state line.[1] It was a short distance west of a cabin Sam Clemens and his pal Cal Higbie had used a few years earlier as they explored the Mono Basin and boated on Mono Lake.[2]

After another ten miles riding south through open sagebrush country along the eastern edge of the Mono Basin, they passed through Dobie Meadows and sage-covered foothills northwest of the Glass Mountains. They rode on into Adobe Valley, where Burke and Jones had told them they would find water and ample grass for the horses.

Hidden at the western edge of the Great Basin, Adobe Valley is what many imagine to be the real "Old West," that magical place of a thousand western movies; the place Zane Grey described in his novels, where the sage glows orange and fades to purple in the sunset. It's a vast, open land of sage, rabbit brush, and, here and there, a lonesome pine.

The valley is surrounded by mountain ranges, one of which blocks the view of the Sierras, which are no more than twenty-five miles west. For geologists, it's an area dominated by extensional transtension between the western Great Basin and the Sierra Nevada.

Reddish, mesa-like canyon walls provide color. Small streams roll out of the canyons into the flat, lonely valley to form meadows that have fed hundreds of wild horses for two hundred years and more. The remains of way stations constructed in the 1860s are reminders that it was once a place where freight wagons, stagecoaches, ranchers, and cowboys and their herds stoked the commerce of the Eastern Sierra, and that it was a source of food and other necessities for the mines around Aurora, Bodie, the White

---

[1] Today's California State Route 167 and Nevada State Route 359 between Lee Vining and Hawthorne.

[2] Twain's *Roughing It* is dedicated "To Calvin H. Higbie, of California, An Honest Man, a Genial Comrade, and a Steadfast Friend. THIS BOOK IS INSCRIBED By the author In Memory of the Curious Time When We Two Were Millionaires for Ten Days."

Mountains, and myriad other areas lying within fifty miles in most every direction.

Dusty roads are now being swallowed by vegetation and eroded by wind and water in a return to nature. Remnants of corrals, sawmills, broken wagon wheels and axles, rock-lined irrigation ditches, and other implements of once bountiful life are scattered about; all—like the roads—on a slow march to oblivion.

But when the convicts entered the valley, the stations were active with travelers seeking rest and refreshment. The toll road to the Owens River had regular rider, wagon, and livestock traffic. Timber-men combed the hills and felled the trees that fed the milling operations that provided the lumber for mine shafts and the homes, churches, and saloons of the area's mining towns. Teamsters hauled the timber. Ranchers and their families fed themselves and sold their hay and root crops and prospered. The pioneering families—Shaw, Dexter, McLaughlin, Watterson, Parker, Evans—and their descendants played a significant part in the history of the region.

Far-off dust clouds generated by animals and wagons served as warning signs. However vast and lonely it may have seemed at first glance, the valley held danger for wanted, desperate, starving men dependent for their lives and freedom on tiring horses. Whether they should risk exposing themselves by continuing along the wagon road was questionable.

As they emerged from the hills, they could see the main Adobe way station with its unique red-rock, circular corral a mile off to the southeast. As they rode well clear of the station, skittish wild horses descended from the ancient Iberian breed ridden by Spanish conquistadores eyed them warily. Jones pointed at the fourteen-thousand-foot eminence of White Mountain in the distance behind the Benton hills. He raised a fist in triumph as he told the men that Bishop Creek was in the valley right below the mountain.

What they needed was to rest and be ready for what might soon confront them. They figured that by now Poor's body had been found, and they thought it probable that lawmen in Bishop Creek had been alerted. They perceived danger behind and danger ahead.

Passing around a line of cliffs, they got back on the wagon road and in a couple of miles stopped in a verdant meadow where the road crossed Adobe Creek. It was a bucolic relic in a sea of sage and sand. They dismounted to let the animals nibble the sweet grass and drink. The men bathed and relaxed in sun-warmed waters where the stream eddied in the shallows near the banks.

Ahead was the last major physical obstacle they would face: the Glass Mountains, at over eleven thousand feet in elevation, a range of lava flows, domes, and pyroclastic flows created in volcanic eruptions eight hundred thousand to two million years before. Four or five deep canyons led toward the crest. Jones and Burke knew that trails up all the canyons could get them over to the Upper Owens River. The question was which route to take. Which would be the quickest? Which would give passage with the least likelihood of being seen?

They pitched camp the in trees on a ridge above the foot of Dexter Canyon, where Dexter Creek met Adobe Creek. They had been up most of Tuesday night and all day Wednesday, riding hard and on steady alert. They decided to lie low for a day or two and see if they could scare up some food. They hadn't eaten anything substantial for three days, their last full meal having been dinner in prison the previous Sunday. Grass was plentiful for the animals; as for the men, there wasn't much. The husks of pine nuts, not quite ripe, hung on the trees and could be knocked off and baked in a campfire to open the cones. There were a few red berries ripened in the September sun. But they couldn't shoot deer or other game for fear of revealing their position.

Jones ripped the collar off the shirt he had taken from Billy Poor. He threw the collar and one of Poor's gloves into the brush near the Dexter Canyon trail.

On Thursday the men started up Taylor Canyon, the route Jones and Burke decided was the safest route over the mountains to the Upper Owens and Long Valley. It was not nearly as heavily traveled as routes farther to the west. As the trail steepened, it became obvious that the horses needed more rest if they were to make it over the crest and down the rugged slopes above the Owens River. Two of the animals limped, and all had foxtails and briars tangled in their fetlocks.

Late Thursday a man later identified as convict Charlie Jones appeared at Hightower's sawmill on the slopes of the mountains four miles east of the Taylor Canyon trail. He begged food for what he claimed were a group of starving prospectors camped in the woods, one of them barefoot. He was given bread, meat, and salt. Reports of this appearance by Jones reached authorities in Benton late Friday.

The group most likely spent Thursday and Friday nights near the tops of the ridges just northwest of the highest point of the Glass Mountains. Hide out for a day or two and maybe the law, not having tracked them, would figure they had headed somewhere else; that was the strategy, at least for the moment. They spread out and moved around, finding safe campsites near the meadows and springs dotting the ridges. Lookouts were posted with long-range views down canyon and out into Adobe Valley.

It's also possible that rather than take the trail up Taylor Canyon, the convicts rode much farther west, followed a wagon road over the top of the ridges at the headwaters of McLaughlin Creek, and descended to the Upper Owens River through McLaughlin Canyon. That was probably the route of the main Aurora and Owens River Wagon Road. However, it's doubtful they took that route. McLaughlin Canyon is nearly seven miles west of the more direct Taylor Canyon route to Long Valley and the Upper Owens River and, eventually, to Bishop Creek. Moreover, it's unlikely that Jones would have ridden a worn-out horse on a twenty-two-mile round trip from McLaughlin Canyon to Hightower's sawmill where he'd begged for food.

Early maps show a trail up Taylor Canyon, through McGee Meadows, and over the top of the range just a mile from Glass Mountain Peak. A century and a half later the trail is well marked and remains a direct route to the Owens for a rider. It could have been utilized by wagons; it was easily passable by horses.

On the Owens River side, the trail descends through O'Harrel Canyon, where a quarter of the way down it meets a logging road that is still in good shape. The road leads down out of the canyon in a beeline across the valley to a bridge at what later became the Turner Ranch. From there, it heads to Hot Creek and the Casa Diablo volcanic area, the areas the convicts were known to have traversed.

The Aurora posse combed the hills and trails between the Elbow and Aurora and between Aurora and the Glass Mountains for two days. They learned from an Indian that the convicts had been seen in Adobe Valley "near Dexter's." They sent reports back saying they had conclusive evidence that Billy Poor was alive; they had found one of his gloves and his collar. Finding no other sign of the convicts, however, and with his men fatigued and their horses worn, Deputy Palmer decided to end the chase. The distraught Horace Poor begged them to "for God's sake make the effort," but he relented when only one other man agreed to go on.

Palmer wrote a note dated "Adobe Meadows, September 22 [Friday]" to Mono County deputy sheriff George Hightower at Benton Hot Springs. He dispatched a member of his posse, J. S. Mooney, to ride fifteen miles to deliver the message.

The note informed Hightower that four or five escaped convicts from the Nevada State Prison were somewhere in the hills back of Adobe Meadows and were likely to head over into Long Valley. If Hightower could raise a posse, he might be able to intercept them. Palmer opined that the horses the convicts were riding would give out soon. He also told Hightower that the convicts had Billy Poor with them to use for their own protection and that the posse should be careful not to harm him. Palmer added that the reward was $500 for each man taken.

Hightower rounded up citizens from the Benton area to form a posse. Jim McLaughlin and Henry Devine departed immediately for Adobe Meadows to guide the Aurora men to Hightower's sawmill in the Glass Mountains. The four other men who eventually joined the group included Robert Morrison, a young man who owned a mercantile store in Benton Hot Springs and served as a Wells Fargo agent.[3]

---

[3] A story written ninety years after the fact states that the convicts took provisions from and molested McLaughlin's wife at her home in McLaughlin Meadows. (See the *Album*, "Times and Tales of Inyo-Mono," no. 111, no. 3, p. 18.) There was no mention of that alleged incident in contemporary news stories or in later publications. Moreover, the story states that when McLaughlin returned home that night, he was incensed and "formed a posse of ten men and two Indian trailers." That was not the case. The posse, which included McLaughlin, had already been formed in Benton by Mono County deputy sheriff George Hightower on the recommendation of Esmeralda authorities.

At his sawmill the next day, Hightower's party took lunch while waiting to hear what the Aurora group could tell them. By then they had been informed that a man who had shown up at Hightower's mill to beg for food was probably one of the convicts. After the briefing they set out at mid-afternoon to search the canyons.

In his pamphlet on the Convict Lake affair, Williams (p. 17) states that "Alpers" joined the posse when it reached Long Valley. That was not the case. The first of the Mono County Alpers, Frederich P., was born in Germany in 1874, migrated first to Minnesota, and finally reached the Eastern Sierra in the late 1880s or the 1890s. He didn't purchase the Thompson Ranch in upper Long Valley until 1906, according to Frederich's grandson, Tim Alpers, a prominent Mono County citizen. Following in the footsteps of his grandfather and his father William, Tim operated the Alpers Ranch, which still bears his family name, until 2008. He is widely known for the "Alpers trout," a hearty fish bred and raised in a hatchery the Alpers family constructed in meadows along the Upper Owens River where the runs were natural instead of concrete-lined, like most modern hatcheries. Today, anglers plying the fruitful waters of Mono County seek the elusive fighting "Alpers."

The convicts began the fateful ride to the Upper Owens and Long Valley late on Saturday, September 23, 1871. As they topped a last ridge at nearly ten thousand feet, the towering eastern escarpment of the Sierra Nevada came into view fifteen miles distant. The floor of the valley lay nearly three thousand feet below.

They could see the dark, craggy face of the peak called Monte Diablo across the valley,[4] a striking feature of that part of the four-hundred-mile-long Sierras. Below was the U-shaped bowl that held the lake called Wit-So-Nah-Pah by the indigenous peoples. To the right were sheer cliffs created when tectonic action uplifted the mountains, and rock was torn eons later from the side of Laurel Mountain by the glaciers that carved out the canyon and lakebed.

The devil mountain became their guidepost. They knew the main road from Casa Diablo to Bishop Creek ran below it. The mountain was a constant reminder that their journey was nearly over. Their hopes rose as it grew near.

---

[4] Variously "Devil Mountain" or "the Devil's Mountain. The 12,241 foot peak is now called Mount Morrison.

THE FATAL AFFAIR IN MONTE DIABLO CANYON

The wild horses of Adobe Valley. (Courtesy of Gail and Nigel Smith)

Remains of the corral at the site of the Adobe Valley way station, constructed in the 1860s. The wooden portion of the structure utilized square nails. The pinkish rock structure is about 200 ft. in diameter. (Courtesy of Gail and Nigel Smith)

Mt. Morrison (Monte Diablo) in the late spring; elevation 12,241 ft. Because of views like this, peak baggers like to call the mountain the Great White Fang.

Courtesy of Rollie Rodriguez

Mount Morrison in the winter with fog. (Courtesy of Rollie Rodriguez)

They guided the tired horses carefully down the steep road through O'Harrel Canyon and emerged onto a broad sage-covered plain in Long Valley, where cattle grazed along the banks of the Upper Owens River. Crossing the river in a meadow area, they followed the river road south a few miles and then branched off on a trail along aptly named Hot Creek.

They passed deer standing in the broad, steamy creek, feeding on vegetation that rode the surface, and they dodged gaping holes filled with roiling mud. The creek itself at times roiled and boiled, and steam from a geyser rose above the ridges off to the west. It was a land of volcanic action, the magma in a cauldron a mere mile below their feet. They were entering the land called Casa Diablo. As they approached it from Hot Creek, the dark visage of Monte Diablo loomed far above, ice and snow visible deep in the myriad chimneys of its vertical face.

It was late afternoon and the horses were exhausted again, laming up, slowing progress. Jones and Burke suggested they hole up at the lake at the base of the mountain and ride the remaining thirty miles to Bishop Creek the next day.

The trail crossed over a glacial moraine—a small mountain—that marked the boundaries of the canyon below the lake. They rode cautiously, making frequent stops to watch behind. A rider trailing them from Hot Creek off to the north would be easily spotted in the intervening two miles of open country. Anyone coming from Long Valley out to the east would also be seen. There were six pairs of searching eyes. Given ensuing events, it's likely they indeed spotted a rider.

They set up camp below the basin holding the mile-long lake, where the creek meandered through willows and meadows and occasional groups of tall pines. They were surrounded on three sides by mountains that seemed to rise right out of the lake. The peak of Monte Diablo, at over 12,000 feet, loomed nearly a vertical mile above. Rounded white rocks stuck high on the flanks of the steep sides of the lake basin—left there by flowing ice and out of place against the dark rock of the mountain proper—gave evidence of the power, depth and enormous weight of the glaciers that carved out the lake and piled up the massive moraines.

The convicts had found an ideal resting place. A sentry could be posted on a nearby knoll. The camp spots they chose were hidden from view, and anyone entering the basin from the canyon would have to cross open areas within easy range of Henry rifles. The meadows along the creek provided fodder for the horses.

Spirits were higher than they had been since the escape. The men scattered to gather wood for campfires and to pick berries at the lake. There was little else to eat, but finally, after nearly a week of fear and fatigue, hunger and thirst, food was of less concern. The morrow would offer new life. The fantasies of men locked away in prison, far from friends and freedom and without the small choices daily life on the outside offers, were soon to become reality.

Morton and Black throw horse blankets on grassy spots softened by pine needles. They find an Indian fire pit and stoke up a fire as night falls.

"Morton, you think it's over?" Black looks at Morton and waits, but there's no reply. "You know, as we was riding up the canyon I was thinking about the farm in Ohio and growing up. You think I can get back there?" He pauses. "But maybe it's no use. They're probably all dead."

Moses Black had come west to find a life for himself. The farm wouldn't support him and his brethren. In days of desperation and economic depression in the East, he'd been thrust out on his own, still in his teens. A large, lumbering man of modest intelligence, his strength and endurance, and unfortunately his gullibility, made him a natural worker for the avaricious mine owners who took every advantage they could of the men they hired. In the habit of drinking his meager wages away on payday and owing more than he could pay back to taverns and landlords in Nye County in Nevada, he'd stolen enough money to get sent to prison for seven years by a zealous prosecutor and a hanging judge.

Black had been in prison just a week when Chapman and Morton convinced him to join them in the escape. Had he remained in his cell, he'd have been paroled in less than two years. Now his fate is beyond his control.

"Damn it," Morton says, shaking his head as if to wake himself from deep thought. "Black, we're safe now. Don't you get it? Quit worrying. Bishop Creek's just down the hill."

Morton pauses and sighs audibly as if letting loose his demons. "I can feel it already. We're free men." He grins and flashes a thumb-up.

"Where do we want to go from here? I guess Ohio is too far." Black is downcast.

Morton turns and stands with his back to the fire, reaching his hands out behind for warmth. "Well, I guess I'd like to go back home too. But it's a long way, and I goddamn sure ain't taking the road east back through Elko and finding myself in front of that bastard judge again." He pauses and spits out a wad. "They'd jail me over in White Pine too." He looks skyward then at Black. "Like I told you, maybe the best thing is go down around the mountains and get ourselves over to the big valley and hire us out. Make our mark and then decide where we go."

He snaps dead branches from a tree and throws them on the pile by the fire. "You know, Black, its warm all the time over there in California. All you need to do to eat is pick something."

"Yeah, I know about the pickings," Black says. "That'd be something all right."

Black gets up slowly, a knee at a time, and walks into the darkness. He brings back a rotted log and throws it on the fire. Sparks cascade upward into the starry night and the devil mountain creates a vast, black gap against the universal expanse. He looks at Morton and then back at the fire and lets out a long breath as he slumps heavily to the ground.

"I mean to stick with you, Morton," he says, mumbling like he has a lump in his throat. "I could probably still up and walk back to Carson, maybe let a posse somewhere take me, but now I'm afraid. That dead mail rider back there is what scares me. I don't want to be hung." His voice tails off in the crackle of the fire. "I don't want to sound like no bawling calf."

Morton kicks at a log sticking out of the fire. "Buck up, now, buck up! Ain't no end of the world. I told you we're free men tomorrow the minute we're down the hill to Bishop Creek."

He leans over the fire and talks at Black, softly, like he's letting out a secret. Firelight and shadow flicker across his bony face; lines of weariness surround his eyes. "You know, I don't give a damn about the rest of them we're riding with. You and me are out of there as soon as we grub up. Get it? We're gone." His voice rises as he gestures with his head. "We don't need them people."

Black sidles over against a boulder warmed by the fire. He pulls down his hat and closes his eyes. "Okay, let's just get over to that valley."

Morton stays awake, nudging the fire with a stick to keep the coals hot, throwing on pine branches from time to time. He's glad he's out of prison, but he regrets following Charlie Jones. He told Black about California to boost his spirits, but he's not sure that's the best way to go.

Maybe we'd be better off to go east out past the White Mountains into the desert. Maybe hole up with Chapman and the boys at Silver Peak and work the mines for a while.

He trusts Black and needs him. If east is where they head, two men can better face the bleakness of the Esmeralda desert or the valleys and ranges of the Great Basin.

He moves his blanket to a grassy spot by the creek, away from the dying fire, and lies with his hands behind his head. He lapses into reverie as he gazes at the stars hanging in the moonless sky. It feels like the black nights of his cowboy days, camping alone in the valleys of the outback, where the stillness seemed audible and a primal dread so often coursed through his fatigued brain. He falls into a fevered sleep of shapeless, colorless dream imagery as new light begins to cap the peaks off to the east.

2
Morrison Spots the Convicts

The Hightower posse set out to find the convicts' trail on the afternoon of Saturday, September 23, the day after the Esmeralda deputy's note reached Hightower, and just about the time the convicts reached Long Valley. They would have four or five hours' pursuit time before dark. The men were familiar with the routes up the canyons, and they knew their horses would be much faster than the beaten animals the convicts were riding. The only question was where and how soon they would overtake their quarry. If they didn't take the convicts before dark, they would hole up for the night at the McGee ranch on the west side of Long Valley at the base of the Sierras. The assumption was that the next morning's pursuit would take them south toward Bishop Creek. They figured the convicts would be trapped between them and parties coming up the grade from the Owens Valley.

Although newspaper accounts agree that Robert Morrison was the first to see the convicts, it's unclear whether he rode with the main body of the posse and where he was when he spotted them. The likelihood is that he watched from a distance as they crossed the sagebrush flat after leaving Hot Creek and rode up into Monte Diablo Canyon. There would have to have been enough daylight for him to see some distance. This indicates he was hours ahead of the posse.

One possibility is that Morrison never rode from Benton Hot Springs with Hightower and the other men when they left to meet the Aurora men at Adobe Meadows. Instead, he might have been instructed to take the Benton Crossing Road around the southeast end of the Glass Mountains, through Watterson Canyon, and then across Long Valley. As a Benton merchant supplying ranches in the area, he'd have been familiar with that route.

Had he started riding the day Hightower posse left for Adobe Valley or in the morning of the day the convicts broke camp after their last night in the Glass Mountains, he'd have been at a point where he could watch them cross the upper portions of Long Valley. The dust kicked up by their horses would have been visible for miles. His instructions would have been to follow and observe, not to engage, and to meet the main body of the posse at the McGee ranch on Saturday night.

Alternatively, Morrison could have been instructed to search up Taylor Canyon from Adobe Valley while other men in the posse spread and searched the other canyons. He could have taken the trail up Taylor Canyon at a fast clip, spotted the convicts' trail on the ridge, and followed it to a point where he had good views of Long Valley. He could have spotted the convicts from up there, followed them at a safe distance, and observed them as they started up the canyon to the lake at the base of Monte Diablo.

Whichever route he took, based on what happened the next day, it's likely the convicts saw Morrison sometime during the day.

Morrison was in a pensive mood. Being off by himself gave him time to think of the dangers he might face. He was to be married the next week to the sister of Henry Devine of Benton, one of the men in the posse. Strangely, he had his wedding clothes with him. Perhaps he had a premonition because he stopped and buried a saddlebag with the clothes at a location he disclosed to a posse member later at the McGee ranch. That he felt the need to tell someone indicates that Morrison had been alone when he buried his clothes and later spotted the convicts.

At McGee's that evening, Morrison reported that the convicts were holed up north of McGee's in Monte Diablo Canyon. Rather than wait and ambush the convicts as they passed McGee's or let them go on toward certain capture in or near Bishop Creek, Hightower's decision was to ride up the canyon the next morning. He reasoned that the convicts knew they would be seen should they try to ride through the open valley past the McGee ranch in the daylight hours. Therefore, he believed they would rest their horses and travel the remaining thirty miles to Bishop Creek toward dusk on

Sunday. There would be ample time then to trap them in the canyon in the morning.

3
The Morning Hours

On Sunday morning, September 24, 1871, Charlie Jones woke before dawn, just as Leander Morton was drifting off. Feelings of dread came over him, telling him to leave on the double. He roused Morton and told him he was headed off to meet his friends in Bishop Creek. He'd round up horses and supplies and meet Morton and the others there. Without waiting for Morton to protest, he took a pistol and shotgun and saddled up as the rays of the rising sun gave an orange tint to snow patches in gullies near the top of Monte Diablo. That he and the others had seen Morrison the day before would explain why Jones hightailed it.

Jones would never be seen again by the convicts who had trusted and followed him, by lawmen, or by anyone who would admit to having seen him. No one would definitively account for his whereabouts or his fate. It's likely he met his friends in Bishop that day and was given provisions before disappearing into history. It may be that his pen pal, Mrs. Luna Hutchison, was there with a fresh horse, just as he had requested in his letters to her.

If in fact he went to Bishop Creek, Jones would have had to pass by the McGee ranch. For whatever reason, he wasn't seen. It may be that he rode far enough out into the valley below the ranch that he wasn't noticed. Or perhaps he saw the posse coming and hid in the willows along Monte Diablo Creek.

Jones was probably a psychopath; he was a killer not known to express remorse for his deeds, emotionless, a man who, sensing trouble, deserted the men who had relied on his leadership. He had stabbed a man to death in White Pine, had killed Matthew Pixley in the gun battle at the prison, and, along with Leander Morton, had murdered and mutilated the body of defenseless Billy Poor. His purposeful boasting about Poor's death had enraged John Burke

That he would escape the fate due him is sheer irony. He had earned the right to swing from the nearest tree.

Fall had just begun to color the aspens and cottonwoods circling the lake. The willows along the creek were still clad in full green. The creek gurgled and danced. Sunlight had begun its trip down from the crest of Laurel Mountain and would soon give sparkle to the mist spun off by the creek's miniature waterfalls. Does and fawns crept down from their mahogany cover on the ridges to drink from the creek. Peace was on the land.

Since the murder of Billy Poor, John Burke and Tilton Cockerill had kept off by themselves. They began to stir as morning warmth found its way under the pines to where they slept. The frost had burned off, and they were hungry. Burke walked down to the creek to tell Roberts they were headed back up to the lake.

Roberts, Morton, and Black were lying under horse blankets, trying to keep warm even as sunlight spread over the canyon floor. As Morton woke from fitful sleep, he began to think through the day ahead and the dangers it might bring. It crossed his mind that the law in Bishop Creek would have figured out that Jones was headed that way, and maybe word of the murder of Billy Poor had reached the town. He reckoned the citizenry would be on high alert.

He thought again about skipping Bishop Creek and heading directly for Silver Peak; he was nervous. He roused Black and pointed to the knoll where he would post watch. He armed himself with a Henry and left as Black rolled over and pulled his blanket tighter.

Hightower gathered his men at breakfast and went over his plan. They would ride up the canyon, surprise the convicts with superior numbers, and surround and arrest them. They would take them back to Carson City, riding shackled in wagons, circumventing Aurora to avoid vigilantes. The round trip would take most of a week, but the rewards Nevada's governor had posted would make it worthwhile.

There's little indication that they discussed tactics. There was no apparent plan to spread out going up the canyon or to enter the bowl above the canyon from different directions as they could have.

The prudent move for Hightower would have been to station his men in the hills overlooking the canyon and its access trail and send to Bishop Creek for reinforcements. It may be that the thought of collecting large rewards skewed his judgment.

Surprise, overwhelm with numbers and weapons, and capture; it was a simple plan, rosily optimistic. But it was fatally ill-conceived, largely because it ignored the firepower of the Henry rifles the convicts possessed and because it assumed the convicts would not be ready for battle. As it played out, it was not a plan worthy of an otherwise smart, energetic group of men, all but one of them citizen volunteers. The men were brave and public spirited and could hardly be blamed, but the events of the day would forever cloud the minds of the survivors.

Riding up the hill from McGee's along the main road toward Casa Diablo, the posse passed the Long Valley ranch and after another three miles topped a long hill. At this point, Hightower could have split his men into two groups, with one heading up a draw south of the main canyon and over a ridge into the basin where the convicts were camped. This would have allowed an attack from the convicts' rear, with the advantage of surprise and high ground. Instead he kept the men together and headed for the willows along the creek at the point where it emerged from Monte Diablo (now Convict) Canyon. Rocks, steep embankments, and pine trees and willows would not allow horses passage up the canyon narrows near the creek, so the ride to the basin above the canyon mouth was along a trail at the base of a lateral moraine fifty yards off the creek. The trail coursed through open sage and rocky glacial dregs. There was no cover.

They watched for signs of movement in the thick willows along the creek, guns at the ready. They couldn't see beyond the canyon rim a half-mile above, and they were in plain sight of anyone watching from there.

Robert Morrison rode ahead with Mono Jim, a Paiute tracker Hightower had invited to join the posse.

4
El Diablo Has His Due

From his sentry's perch, Morton spotted Morrison and Mono Jim as they emerged from the canyon. As he hurried to alert Black and Roberts, Roberts heard him yell, "C'mon, c'mon, here they are!" Taken literally, those words indicate that the posse had been expected, as does the fact that Morton had been on early watch.

Morrison, who had reached a ridge that allowed a view of the area below the lake, saw Morton scramble down the hill. At Morrison's signal Hightower and his men spurred their horses toward the top of the canyon. Bill Chalfant in his *Story of Inyo* wrote that the convicts were camped a hundred yards below the "cup-like basin" holding the lake, which means that when the posse reached the top of the canyon, the convicts were maybe two hundred yards upstream.

Morrison dismounted, leaving his horse with Mono Jim. The Indian rode farther along the main trail on a ridge toward the lake, following a trail that is today the main road past the Restaurant at Convict Lake to the lake itself. Morrison, on foot, either wasn't noticed or was ignored by the concealed convicts, who were focused on the larger group emerging from the canyon. He headed for thick willows upstream.

Hightower's mistake was ignoring the terrain. Coming out of the canyon, his men were in the open without cover and within range of Henry rifles. Instead of dismounting, taking firing positions, and advancing slowly, they rode directly into the teeth of danger. They were startled when they spotted two men among the pines across the creek. They charged with pistols raised.

Convict Roberts leapt up at that moment and ran through a clearing in a desperate attempt to reach safety. He pitched headfirst in the direction of Morton and Black, who were in defensive positions. The first shot of the battle rang out, the ball striking Roberts in the shoulder.

Morton yelled at Roberts, "Get into the willows! They'll surround us, and I'll be shot."

Roberts struggled to move. As he flung himself into a patch of willows, he took another shot in the thigh.[5]

Morton and Black joined battle with Henry rifles. Their initial volleys struck four of the horses ridden by posse members, killing outright those ridden by men named Nabors and Calhoun, and wounding horses ridden by Nesmith and Albertson. Calhoun took a shot through the hand as his horse fell. A shot passed through loose clothing at Nesmith's waist.

The convicts were positioned behind large pines. The stream fronting them could not be crossed without exposure, and there was a hill at their backs. By contrast, their adversaries, now retreating in the open, could find only brush, low rocks, and willows for cover, and they had to expose themselves by rising to kneeling positions to have any chance of getting off effective rounds. Pistols, single-shot rifles, and shotguns were no match for Henry rifles. From a military standpoint, it was no contest.

Crawling for cover, rolling into willows and behind creek banks, the posse gradually drew back toward the lip of the canyon. The rapid-firing big guns boomed behind them, red jets blasting from the barrels, the zings of the rounds audible overhead. Over the next three hours, they would make it on foot six miles back to the McGee ranch. Riders were sent south to alert the citizenry of Bishop Creek. Morrison and Mono Jim were expected back at the ranch in due time.

As a battlefield commander, Hightower's failure was to account for all his men when he signaled a retreat. In truth he was a country rancher and sawmill owner with little in the way of leadership experience and none in tactics.

Morton and Black watched as the posse retreated, laughing and taking a few potshots to hurry them along. The seriously wounded Roberts laid in shock.

Black scurried across the creek to see if any of the horses abandoned by the posse could be ridden. He found two pistols dropped

---

[5] Initial reports were that Roberts had been shot in the foot. Subsequent army medical reports showed that the first shot hit him in the shoulder and the second in the thigh.

during the retreat. Morton meanwhile used a torn shirt to stem blood oozing from Roberts's wounds.

During a quiet moment when they were resting and planning their next move, Morton heard something. With a finger across his pursed lips, he gave a palms downward motion for Roberts and Black to be quiet. They soon noticed movement in the brush across the stream and made out a man attempting to keep low as he crawled in their direction. He had apparently heard them but had not fixed their position.

The man in the brush was Robert Morrison.

"There's a brave chap. I don't like to kill him," Morton said, according to an account Roberts later gave. "But that's the kind to kill. Then you won't have any trouble with the cowards."

Black, on hands and knees and then in a crouch, made his way upstream along the creek, hidden from Morrison's view. With a circling gesture with his arm, he signaled Morton that he would attack Morrison from the rear. He crossed the creek and headed back downstream, cocked rifle in hand. He walked within a few yards of where Morrison was lying in the high sage. He realized his nearly fatal mistake when he heard the explosion of Morrison's pistol. It had misfired.

Black returned fire immediately. The ball struck Morrison in the midsection. Morrison slumped onto his side, appearing to Black to be unconscious or dead. After watching a few seconds, Black put the rifle down, drew a pistol, and walked over to take Morrison's weapon.

Morrison stirred. Despite the agony of a shattered hip, he tried to rise and steady himself enough to get off a shot, but he fell back.

As Black walked up to him, Morrison said, "Hold on." He raised a hand and reflexively turned his head away. Black fired a ball into the back of Morrison's head with no more care than if he was putting a wounded, bawling calf out of its misery.

Morton and Black quickly scoured the area. In addition to Morrison's rifle and pistol and the two pistols previously picked up by Black, they found three other weapons. They retrieved their mounts and started to ride up to the lake to find Burke and Cockerill.

Mono Jim, who had been stationed behind a small hill removed from the battle scene, saw them coming and thought they were members of the posse. According to Roberts, recalling later what Black told him, Mono Jim yelled, "Three men. He stop in willow. He got no gun."

Black yelled back, "Show him to me, and I'll shoot him!"

Mono Jim rode quickly up to Black. He dismounted, but as he was pointing across the neck of Black's horse toward where he had seen the three men, he discovered his error, probably by noticing Black's prison pants. Black shot him in the back as he wheeled to run. As he rolled forward, he managed to draw his pistol and shoot at the horses Morton and Black were riding. Then he fell unconscious. Morton dismounted, strode over with a cocked pistol, and shot him point-blank in the face.

A posse member later gave his version of the battle to the *Inyo Independent*. He said that shots were exchanged for twenty minutes until the convicts finally retreated upstream under the cover of willows. The men in the posse, he said, took three of the convicts' horses and followed them upstream. They watched as the convicts "went up to our guide—brave Mono Jim—who was holding Morrison's horse as he was instructed to do. One of them went up close to him, and as he stepped forward fired two shots from a six-shooter, killing him instantly."

He said the convicts took the two horses held by Mono Jim and continued toward the lake. Someone above yelled, and two more shots were heard. "Being so totally unmatched in point of arms," he said, "we had to return." When asked later by a reporter, he assumed that Morrison had been hit in the first seconds of the battle.

The man's description of the battle doesn't ring true. It makes it sound as if the posse was in control of the battlefield when it was not, and the time sequence leaves no room to account for the death of Morrison. In fact, as Roberts's account indicates, the convicts were able to wander around the battlefield and pick up weapons discarded by the posse before Morrison was killed. This is buttressed by the finding that one of the gunshot wounds Morrison received— the one that killed him outright—was from the pistol of a member of the posse.

The man who gave the rather strange account didn't say why he and the men with him didn't shoot at the outnumbered convicts before or after they killed Mono Jim. If his statement was accurate, the convicts and Mono Jim were in plain sight. Moreover, since the convicts were firing powerful rifles that had brought down horses and wounded a man in the opening salvos, the story that the posse was able to get close enough to the convicts to take their horses doesn't make sense.

It sounds like an attempt to rationalize the events of the day, or perhaps it was the false memory of a man traumatized by what he had experienced. As to the last two shots the man who gave this account heard, in all likelihood he and the others were headed down the canyon on foot when they heard the shots that killed Robert Morrison.

A coroner's inquest and court trial would have ferreted out the truth. Neither was held because of the actions of citizens in the days ahead.

Morton and Black set about planning their next move. They had problems, and they had choices. The first of many problems was that they were dependent on tired horses for escape. Since they had purposely shot the horses from underneath the men in the posse, later events indicate they were left with the same animals they had ridden hard for well over a hundred miles.

This was a severely limiting factor. It would be impossible now to change course and head for Silver Peak; the animals couldn't possibly go that far without days of grazing and rest. On the other hand, they couldn't delay leaving because their location was known, and they were starving.

They had other choices. For example, they could have ridden out of the canyon and turned toward the remote, unpopulated areas of the Sierras a few miles northwest, the opposite direction from Bishop Creek. There they could have grazed the horses and killed game for an indefinite period, and they likely would have found their way through Mammoth Pass to California's Central Valley and freedom.

Another limiting factor was Roberts and his severe wounds. He had dire need for medical attention. Since Morton and Black would abandon him later, twice, the question in retrospect is why they didn't leave Roberts at the lake and let him be taken by the men they knew would return to search for Morrison.

Whatever their reasons, they decided to leave the canyon at once and proceed to Bishop Creek, where they hoped to find Charlie Jones and his friends. The effect of the lack of nourishment on the brain no doubt affected their decision, for Bishop Creek was the worst possible choice. They eventually understood that, because the following day they would make an equally rash, last-minute decision to avoid Bishop Creek by trying to cross through the Sierras to the Central Valley by way of an impassable canyon.

The gun battle—the *Inyo Independent* called it "the fatal affair in Monte Diablo Canyon"—had been a rout. El Diablo had his due that day.

5
Escape to Silver Peak

Burke and Cockerill were at the lake picking currants when they heard the sounds of battle. They concealed themselves and waited. Not knowing that Charlie Jones had left earlier and wasn't in the battle, they wanted no part of him and his murderous ways.

Burke was the one man in the group who had dared take on Jones; moreover, his conscience wouldn't let him kill a man. Cockerill, the train robber, had taken a passive role in the prison escape and ride south. Neither wanted want to be captured with the murderers Jones and Morton. If taken separately, each would at least have a chance to tell his story and place the blame where it belonged. They had rehearsed their stories; under the right circumstances, they would have a reasonable chance of avoiding execution.

During the ride south they had decided to leave the other men and head east to Silver Peak after reprovisioning with the help of Jones's friends at Bishop Creek. Silver Peak was famous as one of the most lawless towns in the West, which is why it was their destination. After the sounds of battle quieted, they decided to head there directly. Bishop Creek would now be too dangerous.

They rode up a bare ridge east of the point where Monte Diablo Creek poured out of the lake. They could have been seen by Morton, Roberts, and Black, but they no longer cared. They topped the ridge and rode down into Long Valley, striking the main road two miles north of the McGee place. At that time, Hightower and his men were struggling to get back down through Monte Diablo Canyon.

Burke and Cockerill took the most direct route toward Silver Peak. They rode across the open spaces of Long Valley, along the Benton Crossing Road up through what Watterson Canyon, and on to the Benton area. It was the route the cortege would follow the next day taking Morrison's body back to his home. After circling Benton, they rode north in Benton Valley, finally crossing the Nevada state line at a high pass that dropped them into the upper reaches of the western Great Basin. They proceeded around the north end of the White Mountains[6] before turning south into the mining country on the eastern flank of the range.

It was country Burke, the teamster, knew well. The mines in the area—Queen Cyn, Red Rock, F&L and Morgan, among others—were so isolated and difficult to reach that he figured he and Cockerill would be safe for a while.

They lingered for two weeks, doing some hard-rock mining and earning enough for food and fresh supplies, but they knew that soon someone would hear of the prison break, of Billy Poor, or of the incident at Monte Diablo. They had to move on.

They traded work for fresh horses and headed east across Nevada's Fish Lake Valley on a direct course for Silver Peak. The town, a supply point for dozens of rich mines in the area, was twenty miles away on the far side of the Silver Peak Range. They would work there a few weeks before stocking up and heading out into a desert where no sane man would try to track them.

Esmeralda sheriff John Helm and deputies John Ludwig and John Wheeler had ridden from Aurora to Bishop Creek at the

---

[6] The range includes California's White Mountain Peak, at 14,252 feet in elevation one of the highest peaks in the continental United States, and Boundary Peak, at 13,147 feet the highest peak in Nevada. The indigenous people called White Mountain "Paiute Peak," as many locals, Indians and non-Indians alike, still do.

request of Billy Poor's family, searching for signs of the young man along the way. On learning that Burke and Cockerill were still on the loose, Helms thought they might be headed for Silver Peak. His suspicions were confirmed when he learned that two unfamiliar men had recently shown up and worked up a grubstake at mines in the White Mountains. Interviews at the mines convinced Helm that the two men were indeed headed for Silver Peak.

As Helm and his deputies rode the stage road from Fish Valley into the Silver Peak Range, Ludwig recalled that there was a deserted ice house a mile or so up a side canyon. It would be a good place for men to hide out. They struck tracks at the mouth of the canyon and shortly came upon an abandoned camp by a creek behind the ice house where a few potatoes, some flour sacks, and a blanket were scattered by a smoking fire pit.

Fresh tracks pointed up the canyon toward Red Mountain. The men split to ride through draws up both sides of the mountain. Not far from the top of a ridge leading to the peak, Ludwig spotted Cockerill peering over a rocky ledge. When Ludwig pointed his Spencer rifle, Cockerill stood and threw up a hand, but he quickly dropped out of sight. A few minutes later, after Ludwig's calls that he was surrounded and could either surrender or die, Cockerill appeared with arms held high. Burke was close behind, arms raised.

It was October 11, 1871, twenty-four days after the prison escape. Burke and Cockerill had traveled at least 350 miles.

They denied having been with the Jones party and claimed to know nothing of the death of Billy Poor. Knowing these were lies, Helm's deputies talked openly about a quick lynching right there on the mountain. The sheriff refused, saying it was his duty to take the men to Carson City where they would collect reward money worth a couple of months' wages.

On the return trip, Helm locked the convicts in his jail in Aurora for a night. They were put under guard to prevent citizens fuming over the death of Billy Poor from taking them off for a hanging. During the night, several attempts to get at them were rebuffed, one local offering $500 in gold coin to a guard if he would leave for a few minutes.

Burke and Cockerill were turned over to deputy United States marshal James S. Slingerland in Carson City and dressed once again in "slingerland's best." Their prospects were summed up in an article in Carson City's *Daily State Register* that resembled the tongue in cheek prose of former Carson resident Mark Twain.

> First, they will be tried by the United States for robbing the mail by force of arms, and if found guilty, will be hanged. Second, they will be tried by the same authority for killing a mail agent or carrier, and if found guilty will be hanged. Then they will be turned over and tried by the State for the murder of Poor, and if found guilty will be hanged a third time. Then again they will be tried as accessories to the murder of Pixley, and if found guilty they will be hanged the fourth time. And last and least, they will be tried for State Prison breaking, and sentenced to prison for from one to ten years. As they were probably not present at the killing of Morrison and Mono Jim, they may get out of that scrape.

In fact the two men were eventually paroled and disappeared into the fog of time.

CHAPTER 7

Atonement

1
"A Large and Grief-Stricken Circle of Friends Attended the Solemn Ceremony"

The morning after the battle, Hightower, Alney McGee, and several other men rode from McGee's back to Monte Diablo Canyon to search for Morrison, hoping they would find him alive, at worst wounded and holed up with Mono Jim. As they entered the area below the lake basin where the battle had taken place, they spotted Mono Jim's body up the trail where two horses were milling about. Edging warily down toward the creek, they saw a man lying facedown in the sagebrush near a clump of willows. They could tell from a distance it was Morrison, obviously dead.

They buried Mono Jim in a shady spot near where he died. After gathering slugs and shell casings to aid an investigation, they wrapped Morrison in a canvas tarp and tied him across a horse for the trip back to McGee's.

The shot that disabled Morrison had entered his left hip, the ball passing entirely through his body. He'd likely have died from that wound in a matter of hours. Powder marks indicated that the shot that killed him outright was fired at point-blank range, the ball entering the back of his head and exiting above the right eye. The slug near his body had come from the pistol of a posse member.

Hightower sent riders to Benton and Bishop Creek with word of Morrison's death and a warning that the convicts were armed with Henry rifles. Later in the day, a somber cortege set off on the thirty-mile ride to Morrison's home. A wagon drawn by two horses carried his body. The sad, quiet group made its way across the wide valley and through and over the lonely canyons and passes that marked the way. It crossed a last, low pass before descending into Benton Hot Springs where friends and neighbors had gathered. Home a last time, Morrison was dressed in his finest clothes and laid out in his living room in a pinewood casket. Men, women, and children from Benton and the nearby ranches and mines came to pay their final respects to the popular storekeeper.

Sarah Devine, the young lady from Benton soon to have been his bride, was never to see him again. She was 300 miles away in Los

Angeles preparing for the wedding; the distance wouldn't allow her to return in time for the funeral.

Robert Morrison was born in New York, where his Irish immigrant family still resided. One newspaper said he was twenty-six years old when he died, which means he'd have been born in 1845, a year after John C. Fremont and his men blazed the trail that would become a section of the Esmeralda Road followed by the convicts who killed Morrison. That report, however, was incorrect; twenty-six was probably his age when he arrived in Inyo County.

The *Mono County Great Register of 1871*, published by H. S. Crocker and Company of Sacramento, listed the names of county residents who were naturalized, the date they were registered, and their ages and occupations. Morrison, listed as a Benton merchant, was first registered in May 1867. The 1871 register lists his age as thirty. If that was his when he was first registered in 1867, he was thirty-four when he died; if, however, that was his age as of the 1871 listing, he was thirty when he died. Mono County's official records do not have his death certificate.

A website dedicated to Morrison (http://www.robertmorrison.org) states that he was thirty-four when he died. It says his parents had emigrated from Ireland through Ellis Island. Many Morrisons came to this country from Scotland (Morrison is primarily a Scottish name), England, and Ireland in the 1800s. However, Morrison's parents did not come through Ellis Island. The island was not used for immigration screening until designated for that purpose by the House Committee on Immigration in 1890. Its screening functions ended in 1924. The first immigrant to be processed through the Ellis Island administrative center was rosy-cheeked Annie Moore from County Cork, a fifteen-year-old who had come to join her parents.

The *Inyo Independent* said Morrison was one of the earliest pioneers of the Owens Valley, having arrived in Owensville in 1863. "[N]o man in all this country commanded more friends or was held in more universal esteem. How very, very sad will be the terrible tidings" to his fiancée and family.

The funeral services were conducted by the Masons, and a "large and grief-stricken circle of friends attended the solemn ceremony." Morrison was laid to rest on a pleasant hillside a short distance from his home.

2
No Country for Mean Men

*W*ell before Morrison's funeral, the drums of vengeance were sounding. In Bishop Creek rumors had it that certain of the citizenry had aided and abetted the murderous convicts. Luna Hutchison, the lady who had corresponded with convict Charlie Jones, was thought to be among them. So were Cap Smith, Bill Gill, and Jack Horton.

An article in the September 30, 1871, edition of the *Inyo Independent* captured the mood of the people (the emphasis is added).

> Need Hanging
> [T]here are some parties residing round the scene of the tragedy in the upper end of the county who need some attendance at the hands of an outraged community. They not only openly avowed sympathy with the escaped cutthroats, but, it appears from their operations, made efforts to assist them. A gent at Benton thought that the death of Mr. Morrison was a good lesson, and that he would give one Burke the best horse he ever straddled to get away with. Some are charged with lending actual assistance, while still others were so selfish as to refuse to lend guns for use by their pursuers. *We would gently advise these parties to haul in their horns, or this climate may not prove altogether agreeable to their health.*

It can reasonably be assumed that the "gent at Benton" wasn't a popular man, if indeed he hauled in his horns and stayed around long enough to test his reputation after the article made its rounds.

It wasn't a country where the murderers of a young mail rider and a popular merchant would want to be found. Yet this was the hell into which Morton, Black, and Roberts would descend.

With Burke and Jones gone, the leaderless trio had little familiarity with the remaining route to Bishop Creek. They would run a huge risk by going back down to the main road, passing the McGee ranch, and dropping three thousand feet down to the Owens Valley.

It would be thirty miles, much of it through open country. Nonetheless, just about dark on the day of the gun battle, they rode down the canyon and turned south, determined to follow any trails they could find that hugged the eastern flank of the mountains and provided cover. The decision to continue toward Bishop Creek was the first of several mistakes they would make over the next two days.

They were able to ride past McGee's. Hightower and his men, still not knowing the fate of Morrison and Mono Jim, were undoubtedly on the watch. So if the convicts were spotted, they were probably allowed to pass because they were heavily armed and because they were headed into a trap.

After passing through dense aspens surrounding creeks named Hilton and Whiskey by early-day prospectors and cattlemen, they avoided the way station at Rock Creek.[1] They followed a cattle trail[2] south through the rolling hills at the foot of the upper regions of Wheeler Crest and camped in hanging meadows by a creek.

Descending steep trails the following morning they had good views of the green pastures of Round Valley and the sage-covered sand hills marking the way to Bishop Creek. The latter, twelve miles distant, appeared, mirage-like, as an oasis floating in the early fall sky. It was apparent they would be seen if they should ride through the open spaces beyond Round Valley.

They made a fateful decision to head for a rugged, steep-walled canyon slashing into the Sierras five miles away at the far edge of the massive cliffs that form Wheeler Crest.[3] Disorganized, dispirited, starving, and talking openly of lynch mobs, they deluded themselves into thinking the canyon would give them safe passage through the Sierras to California's Central Valley.

Entering Round Valley, they rode along the base of the Wheeler cliffs from spring to spring across rocky alluvial fans. The indistinct

---

[1] Later called Tom's Place.
[2] Called the Ricky Trail, it had been forged over the prior eight years by Sam Bishop and other cattlemen taking their herds up from Bishop Creek in the spring to graze the lush meadows of Long Valley.
[3] They were looking at Pine Creek Canyon. The canyon and the creek flowing through it had not been named by 1871. It was referred to in contemporary accounts as "the canyon above Round Valley" or "the canyon above the Birchim place."

Indian trails took them through horseback-high sagebrush and rabbit and bitter brush. They aimed for the willows marking the creek flowing from their target canyon.

As they entered the canyon and started upward, the going became steep and difficult. The near-vertical canyon walls had spewed avalanches and rockfalls for age upon age, littering the canyon floor with boulders and debris that gave difficult passage for the horses.

Roberts was in a sorry state. Death was no more than a few days away without medical attention. His clothes were caked with blood. He was light-headed, from pain and from the onset of infection caused by specks of his filthy wool prison shirt that had been blasted into his shoulder by the rifle ball. That the ball had passed completely through the shoulder without fragmenting was likely the only thing that had saved him. His crude bandages attracted insects, and every stumble by his tired horse tore at his festering wounds.

After riding nearly five miles and gaining two thousand feet in elevation, the men found to their dismay that they were in a box canyon; it ended at a thousand-foot wall. It looked impossible for horses. Unfit of mind and in dire straits, they decided to try to ride up a faint game trail that hugged the canyon's south wall.

They started through a dense stand of pines and thick underbrush covering a rocky bluff at the foot of the wall, tree branches and thistles tearing at their clothes and the sides of the horses. The trail steepened quickly and took them through dangerous boulder fields and loose, reddish scree. They were soon looking hundreds of feet into the canyon depths. The exhausted horses were frightened and balking; it was hopeless.

Roberts's horse reared and threw him. As the animal turned to charge back down the trail, it slipped over the edge and rolled to its death. Nearly overcome with pain, lying on the ground bruised and battered, Roberts pleaded frantically with Morton and Black to let him ride with one of them.

The two men backed off to talk. They agreed there was no way they could haul Roberts along and get safely down the canyon, let alone manage an escape. Given his weakened condition, they figured he would die no matter what they might do. Saying nothing, they turned back down the canyon. Their horses gave out in the rock fields below. They shot one and abandoned the other and continued on foot, carrying two Henry rifles, several pistols, and heavy loads of ammunition.

They holed up at a spot in the lower reaches of the canyon where they could ambush anyone who should happen to ride near them. They were determined not to be taken alive. The only out now was a long walk through open country to Bishop Creek. The usually cocksure Morton worried more about what fate had in store than at any time since the prison escape.

Forlorn and hungry beyond words, they stoked a campfire and nodded off.

Hours into the night, Black was startled by a plaintive call. It was Roberts. He had stumbled and crawled down the canyon, guided the last half mile by the flickering light of the fire on the canyon walls. Black went into the darkness and carried him back to where Morton sat. Moaning softly, saying nothing, Roberts rolled close to the fire and lost consciousness.

There was no sharp break of day, just a slow enveloping of light from all around. As the shape of the mountains formed, Morton and Black rose to leave, their faces stern and as gray as the morning, their visages blank, as if they were resigned to the vagaries of fate.

Roberts awoke and tried to rise to his feet, but he fell back when his weight shifted to his wounded leg. He cried out in frustration, tearing at his crude bandages in an effort to quell the pain and stop the incessant itching.

Morton and Black filled their canteens and scratched along the stream for something edible. A few minutes after they returned to warm their hands at the fire, Morton beckoned. They picked up their weapons and the ammo-laden saddlebags they would use as rucksacks and walked away.

"He's a goner," Morton muttered.

Roberts heard him and knew it was true. Pain turned to delirium. His mother's pancakes and a cup of hot coffee were in his thoughts as his mind closed down.

Hearing the news from the McGee ranch, John Crough and John Clark of Bishop Creek organized a search party and set out for the hills beyond Round Valley, knowing it was likely the convicts would pass through there. With the help of Indian trackers, they found the convicts' trail and followed it to where it started up the canyon.

Crough and Clark knew they were outgunned. Rather than chance an ambush in the canyon, they alerted ranchers in Round Valley and returned to Bishop Creek with a warning that five or six convicts were headed toward town.

The news was relayed to the US Army post at Camp Independence, forty miles south of Bishop Creek. The post had been established in 1862 to protect miners from Indian raids. Major Harry C. Egbert, the post commander, selected five soldiers to ride with him to locate and arrest the convicts.[4] With a supply of arms for citizens who might want to join forces, the troops were in Bishop Creek within seven hours of the time Egbert was notified.

Egbert found the citizenry of the upper end of the Owens Valley at the ready. Told there were at least five escaped convicts headed that way, he said he would make arrests in short order.

The troops wouldn't be needed. Men who had been trailing the convicts from Carson City, along with several groups from Bishop Creek, had been on the hunt in the valley for two days. The hope was to capture the convicts, return them to prison, and collect the sizeable rewards.

A committee of citizens with other ideas was also being organized.

On Wednesday, September 27, 1871, ten days after the prison escape, three days after the gunfight at Monte Diablo, Morton and Black began the long march to Bishop Creek. As they walked out of the canyon and passed the end of a ridge-like moraine, Morton pointed to groves of trees just visible on the valley floor out to the southeast. He told Black it was maybe ten miles; it wouldn't be long.

After walking a mile down the creek, staying among willows, they turned east as they neared a ranch where they could see activity around a corral.[5] They paralleled the Round Valley Road headed

---

[4] Camp Independence was closed in 1884. Its remains are located just north of Independence, the seat of Inyo County, near where Oak Creek joins the Owens River. Major Egbert, who eventually attained the rank of general, was killed in battle in the Philippines.

[5] It was the Birchim Ranch, at or near an area now called "Forty Acres." The area is still served by Birchim Road.

toward Bishop Creek, staying far enough off the road to be able to duck and hide. The safe haven of their foggy imaginations was now just nine miles away.

Hunger and hope drove them. Cover was so sparse they had to fall prone in the sagebrush to avoid being seen by riders who occasionally passed on the road. Apart from willows along a rock-lined irrigation ditch or the occasional creek flowing out of the Sierras, there was nowhere to hide. At one point Morton told Black he was sure they had been seen.

Limping along, Black cursed aloud, regretting that he'd ever left the prison, talking incessantly, deliriously, of his fear of a lynch mob.

Morton cursed himself for having believed a single word Charlie Jones had ever uttered. And he cursed at Black, telling him to cut the crazy talk, that everything would be okay.

The sun became relentless as the day lengthened. A hot wind began to blow up the Owens Valley, kicking up dust devils. Mucous membranes dried to crust and eyeballs watered. The blue air shimmered as heat rose from the valley floor. There were long stretches with no shade and progress was agonizingly slow. Black was miserable in hobnail prison boots made for quarry work. The ill-fitting boots Morton had taken from the murdered Billy Poor tore at his feet. They shed their shirts as they marched along; their woolen pants were hot and scratchy and grabbed at every bush and thistle. Twice they stopped at irrigation ditches to take off their boots and soak open, bleeding blisters.

They were parched and weak and hungry almost beyond thought; glycogen-starved muscles ached. But their Xanadu drew nearer with each step. They decided to walk to a point within a mile or so of Bishop Creek where they could see buildings. They would hole up and finish the walk at night. When they found the people Jones said would help, they would eat and drink and then pack up and go. Although it had been loose talk before, they decided to head south around the Sierras to enjoy the freedom California's Central Valley would offer. Their expectations grew; their relief was overwhelming.

As they crested a rolling, sage-covered, sandy hill separating Round Valley from the Owens Valley proper, Morton whacked Black on the back. "There it is, Black! There it is!" He raised his fist in triumph as he pointed at a line of trees about a mile away that emerged from the western foothills and extended out to the valley floor. It was Bishop Creek right there in front of them. After a hellish journey of close to two hundred miles, freedom and safety were within their grasp. They were close enough to hear the sounds of barking dogs riding the wind. Black sank to his knees.

Their exultation had scarcely died away when a dust cloud rose behind a knoll between them and the trees. Then the riders appeared, seven of them, moving at a fast pace. Both men dropped and rolled into a swale, but they had been spotted. The horsemen moved to a gallop, straight at them, two hundred yards and closing. Black hastily fired a pistol, and Morton got off two shots, but there was no time to fire the Henrys. The horsemen spread and fired back. Morton yelled at Black to keep down, saying if he rose to shoot he'd be shot dead.

The leader, a man the others called Hubbard, hollered at them to surrender. He yelled that if they dropped their arms he would protect them from the citizens.

Morton stood, hands held high. As Black got up, one of the riders told him to drop the pistol in his waistband. An Indian tracker didn't understand the command and shot at Black, thinking he was reaching to fire the pistol. The ball glanced off the side of Black's head, knocking him semiconscious to the ground with a concussion and severe head wound. Based on a rumor that spread with news of the capture, an exaggerated newspaper account said the ball had passed all the way through his head.

Hubbard demanded to know where the other men were. Morton said they were the only two. Hubbard called back that he knew damn well there were others and that he would find them.

The two men were placed under guard in a cabin at the Birchim ranch where they were given bread and coffee. They were told they would be taken back to Carson City. Black was relieved at hearing he would be returned to prison; Morton was not. The guards, they were told time and again, were there to protect against an attempt by citizens to take them.

"He [Charlie Jones] ran us into a hornet's nest," Morton was quoted as saying. "I prefer being shot rather than to be taken to Carson." The article in the *Inyo Independent* ended with an ominous proclamation (emphasis added): "During this week we shall issue an extra containing the terrible story related by this man [Morton], *and an account of the lynching which the outraged community will doubtless enact, either at Round Valley or Benton.*"

If that wasn't an incitement to a lynch party, it was an acknowledgment of an imminent lynching. The person who wrote the article may have been Pleasant Arthur Chalfant, the editor and publisher of the newspaper and a leading Owens Valley citizen.[6]

Whoever wrote the article had heard that the citizens would "doubtless enact" a lynching, so it's likely he had an idea of who would comprise the lynch party, and he knew they would strike that week. The article appeared Saturday, September 30, 1871, three days after the men were captured. There had been ample time to form a citizens' safety committee.

Morton told his interrogators that the young convict J. B. Roberts had killed Morrison and that Roberts was probably lying dead in the canyon above the Birchim Ranch. He said there were several more escaped prisoners coming toward Bishop Creek. His words were enough to cause warnings to the citizenry to "sleep on their arms."

Four men left to search for Roberts in the canyon. Major Egbert and his army troops set off on a twenty-mile ride to Coyote Canyon in the Palisades region south of Bishop Creek to hunt for six convicts said to be holed up there. Others started the search for two men supposedly seen in the White Mountains.

The newspaper reported that yet another party claimed to have trapped five convicts in an unapproachable canyon but had been

---

[6] Pleasant Arthur "P. A." Chalfant (1831-1901) founded the *Inyo Independent* (now the *Inyo Register*) in 1870. The *Independent* ultimately spawned a series of publications put out by the Chalfant Press. William A. "Bill" Chalfant (1868-1943), P. A.'s son, took over as editor and publisher when his father was elected county assessor in 1887. The younger Chalfant became one of the most respected newspapermen in California. His books, including *The Story of Inyo*, written in 1922 and revised in 1933, and *God, Guns & Ghost Towns*, are recommended reading for anyone interested in the history of the Eastern Sierra. The latter includes a first hand account of the Gold Rush days written by the elder Chalfant that would do honor to Mark Twain. Remarkably, rather than being first written out, the story was composed as Mr. Chalfant stood and meticulously set type.

forced to retreat because of the convicts' superior firepower. That was an erroneous report based on the earlier report of Crough and Clark, the men who two days earlier had tracked Morton, Black, and Roberts to the canyon above Birchim's.

All in all, the count was up to some fourteen escapees said to be on the prowl. In fact, just three had reached the Owens Valley.

Men searching for Roberts in the canyon were sitting by the creek eating lunch when one of them saw movement in the willows just twenty yards upstream. Figuring it was Roberts, the call was to surrender.

Roberts staggered out and fell to the ground. "Boys, I suppose you intend to kill me," he said as a man approached with a rifle. "Give me a cup of coffee, and I am ready."

Roberts had crawled nearly five miles and was four days with little food. His captors reported that exposure and hardship, along with his wounds, had unseated his mind, for he asked if his father and mother were waiting for him in the valley. "How far is it to the nearest house where they have plenty of grub?" he asked.

After his wounds were treated, Roberts was interrogated. Told he'd been fingered by Morton for killing Morrison, he vehemently denied it. He gave his interrogators the details of the battle in Monte Diablo Canyon, how he was wounded early on and unable to join the fray, and how Morrison had crawled toward them and was shot point-blank by Black. He didn't see "who had shot the Indian."

Morton's reaction when he was brought in and confronted by Roberts—he was said to have "blanched and turned color"—convinced the interrogators that Roberts had told the truth.

R. I. Hubbard and A. M. Nesmith, who were at the battle at Monte Diablo and were in the group that captured Morton and Black, had been on the trail of the convicts since the prison break. Hearing from Roberts that Charlie Jones had left before the gun battle and was headed for Death Valley, they left to hunt him down.

Based on Morton's lies and the spread of rumor after rumor, the Owens Valley seemed alive with convicts, all said to be armed and dangerous. Women and children were told to remain indoors. The stories of Morrison's death became more gruesome by the day. Billy Poor, the mail rider from Aurora, was still missing, and rumors (which turned out to be true) spread that he'd been butchered and killed by the convicts. All the while the Paiute tribe was mourning the death of Mono Jim.

One word defined the mood and talk of the citizenry: vengeance. The criminal laws of Nevada and California were for other times and places.

3
The "Trial"

On Sunday afternoon October 1, 1871, two weeks to the day after the prison escape and one week after the shoot-out at Monte Diablo, the cabin door was unlatched and guards led the shackled Morton, Black, and Roberts to a spring wagon drawn by two horses. They were told they were being taken to Carson City. Roberts, getting weaker by the day, would soon die without competent medical care. He was laid out in the bed of the wagon. The stumbling Black was ordered to sit in the bed, and Morton sat shackled by the driver. Armed outriders would protect the prisoners.

If the intent of their captors was to take the prisoners from Round Valley to Carson City, they would have proceeded north toward Casa Diablo. The guards, however, ordered the driver to take the road toward Bishop Creek, nine miles in the opposite direction. Perhaps the purpose, unlikely though it may have been, was to secure supplies, but the move was ill-considered.

The entourage proceeded to Bishop Creek without interruption. At a point not far from a store called "the Jew's,"[7] it was met by a mob of well-armed citizens who rode out from trees lining the roadway. The leader yelled, "Who is the captain of the guard?" A guard replied, "I am. Turn to the left and go on." Rather than turn, the leader raised his rifle and shouted commands as the mob circled the wagon. "These are our prisoners now. They're going to get the

---

[7] Bill Chalfant called it "the Pinchower's store." Others have said it was near "the Brockman corner." Brockman Lane today crosses US Highway 395 in the northern reaches of Bishop.

justice they deserve." Without a show of resistance, the guards moved away. The leader signaled for the wagon to follow.

Morton told the wagon driver, "Give me the reins, and I'll drive after them. I'm a pretty good driver myself." The driver handed the reins to Morton, jumped off the wagon, and disappeared into the trees.

Roberts cried that he wouldn't go with any "goddamn vigilantes," but he was ignored. Black just moaned.

With Morton driving to what he surely knew was likely to be his own hanging, the horsemen and their captives moved a mile north through a meadow to a vacant ranch house. Roberts and Black were placed in a back room where a fire had been started in a rusted potbellied stove. Morton jumped down from the wagon and walked into the house, seemingly without a care in the world. Armed guards stood in the dimly lit room.

Lanterns were strung up in the living area. A "jury" was organized consisting of all present except the guards, and a secretary was appointed to memorialize the proceedings.

Roberts was carried into the room where the jury had convened. As he had when questioned two days earlier, he gave the details of the battle at Monte Diablo canyon and the killing of Robert Morrison and Mono Jim. He described the prison break, the robbery of the coal burner, and the route taken by the escapees. He had figured out that the locals had not yet learned the fate of mail rider Billy Poor, so he played dumb when asked if he knew Poor's whereabouts.

Morton and Black testified separately, giving rehearsed statements similar to what they had first told their captors. Both laid the blame for Morrison's death on young Roberts and the killings at the prison on Charlie Jones. They denied knowing anything about Billy Poor. Morton admitted he killed Mono Jim, apparently thinking the murder of an Indian wouldn't buy him trouble. After a round of hard questioning, the two men were returned to the back room.

The deliberations of the jury were neither long nor deliberate. Convinced by his demeanor and youthfulness, they decided that Roberts was a blameless pawn of Morton and Black and the rest of the gang he had fled south with. They voted to send the eighteen-year-old back to the guard for transport to Camp Independence, where he could get medical attention before his return to prison in Carson City.

The question of whether Morton and Black were guilty, or innocent, or deserved consideration based on extrinsic factors, was not debated. A straw vote was taken immediately after the decision on Roberts. The verdict of "guilty" of the killings of Robert Morrison and Mono Jim was unanimous. The only remaining question was whether to send the men back to prison or to dispatch them locally. There was no dissent to a motion to hang them at once.

A party was sent for lumber. On its return, a scaffold was hastily erected at the west end of the house. One end of a long beam rested on the chimney "while the other was supported by three pieces of scantling resting on the ground." The scaffold consisted of a long crossbeam off the chimney to which two beams were affixed at the other end. The bottoms of the beams were pulled apart to form a triangle, with the ground as the third side. Two ropes were passed over the crossbeam and a wagon driven under.

4
"And Such a Death"

Morton says, "Quit your whimpering, Black. You sound like that bawling calf you're always talking about." He hears the preparations going on outside. "Black, are you ready to die?"

"No! No! This is not the crowd that will hang us. It can't be, Morton, it can't."

"Yes, it is. Don't you hear them building the scaffold?"

Asked by a guard if he wants to stand by the stove, Morton says, "It ain't worth the warming now." He turns to Roberts. "We are to swing, and I mean to have you hung with us if I can. I want company."

Roberts edges closer to one of the guards. He says nothing. His head droops and he sways as he drifts in and out of consciousness.

The hammering outside stops and Black's whimpering grows louder. "It wasn't meant for me to go like this," he says to Morton.

"Life ain't 'meant' to be nothing," Morton says. "What happens just happens, and there ain't a damn thing you can do about it. Now go quiet and take your medicine."

The door is kicked open from the outside and crashes loudly against the inner wall. Four men rush in.

"It's time to go, boys, it's time to go!" one of them shouts, a twisted smile on his face.

Things happen whirlwind fast, as if the hangmen want to get it over as quickly as possible.

Two men grab Black's arms and guide him out to the wagon. As he's hoisted up to stand in the bed he sways dizzily; men reach to brace him. He impulsively runs his tongue over his dry lips. He's ashen, his breathing shallow; he gasps to suck in air.

A man climbs onto the wagon and places a noose around his neck. The rope is slackened enough to make certain it will stop Black's fall just before his feet hit the ground. Sandwiched between the bandages wrapping his head and his dark beard, the circles under his eyes are big and dark. It looks as if he has no eyeballs at all, just holes in a fleshless skull.

After chatting with the guards, Morton walks outside unassisted. Turning the corner, he stops to look at the scaffold. "Boys, you done a good job, a real good job. Best I've seen yet. Just make sure it works the first time." He gives a gap-toothed smile. "You know, it ain't right for a man to swing twice."

He hops onto the wagon and slips the noose dangling next to Black over his own head and makes sure it's fixed firmly around his scrawny neck. He's determined to show he's not a coward.

He turns to the man standing on the wagon. "Tie my hands tight. I don't want to be flailing around when I drop." He turns his back and holds his hands out behind. "And take my collar out from under the rope. Can't hang a man with his collar under the rope now can you?"

Black moans. "I need water."

Morton laughs. "What the hell you want with water now?" He pauses and looks out and says, as if to amuse the crowd that had grown as word spread through the valley, "Course you may need it where you're going."

Asked if they want a preacher, Morton says, "I told the minister what I had to say yesterday, but I guess it ain't proper for a man to be taken off without some religion. If the minister is here, I'd like to have a prayer offered."

There's a lull; quiet comes over the crowd. The executioners mill about for uncomfortable minutes like they've lost track of their purpose or want to forget why they're there.

The preacher Morton had talked with earlier finally steps forward and reaches up to touch him. Head lowered, eyes closed, Morton listens intently.

In a voice that sounds like his larynx is rusted, the preacher offers a prayer directed toward the surrounding mob. He entreats his God to "forgive these forsaken men and take their souls home." Clearing his throat, he speaks louder, defiantly, like he means to teach a lesson to any other sinners within his ken. He quotes an unforgiving passage from Psalms: "For in death there is no remembrance of thee: in the grave, who shall give thee thanks?" He turns to watch men die at his holy hands and the whims of his brethren.

Black's moans roll off with the breeze and fade into the open spaces of the Eastern Sierra.

Morton slowly looks up. "Boys," he says haltingly, "I am prepared to meet my God." He pauses and gazes into the vastness beyond the crowd, moving his head slowly from side to side, taking a last, long look at the world. He takes a deep breath and looks down, head sagging to his chest as the last wave of bravado releases with a sigh. In a quiet voice heard only by those nearest the wagon, he mutters, "But I don't know that there is any god for me."

He turns his back and reaches out his bound hands to shake the hand of a man standing next to him on the bed of the wagon. With a look of horror, the man steps back and jumps to the ground.

Murmurs of "Amen" ripple through the crowd as the horses are prodded and the wagon slowly begins to move.

As if pleading for mercy from his Maker, Black looks skyward as he's pulled backward off the wagon. His moaning is silenced by the rope; his heavy body heaves once and he dies. Had he remained in prison, his minor crimes would have soon gotten him parole.

Morton, a slight, agile man, had worried that he would suffer if the drop of his body didn't kill him quickly. Just as Black falls away, he yells out, turns, and springs high into the air away from the wagon. The hangman's knot violently, audibly snaps his neck, causing a gasp from the crowd. A weird sound from somewhere inside escapes his body, but he dies without moving a muscle.

The crowd quietly milled about after the executions, some men curiously examining the bodies close up, others preferring to just fade from the scene. Morton and Black were left dangling from the scaffold well into the next day, whether as an example to others or as proof to an outraged citizenry that justice had been exacted.

The person who acted as secretary at the trial prior to the lynching returned to the scene that night and described what he saw:

> Morton's face was turned to the light as he was hanging, and in the pale rays of the moon, his countenance, with mouth and eyes tightly closed, presented the appearance of a man in quiet sleep, but it was the sleep of death—and such a death!

A week after the lynching, the *Inyo Independent* rather self-consciously rationalized the event:

> Thus terribly ended the career of crime of two of the murderous prison breakers, and never again shall their hands be stained with the blood of their own fellow man.
>
> Notwithstanding the bad example of mob violence, we have naught but commendation of the entire course taken by the citizens in thus forestalling that stern justice which would otherwise be long-delayed—indeed, it is extremely doubtful whether the regular course of law would *ever* mete out adequate punishment. The judgment, coolness and decision which has characterized all these proceedings must meet the approval of all familiar with the facts.

Morton and Black were buried in a common, unmarked grave at a place known simply as "Jim Shaw's field." Although the location is now not certain, their bones probably lie buried somewhere near US Highway 395 as it exits the city of Bishop headed north.

The lynching remained in the collective consciousness of the community for years. A generation later, in the mid-1890s, a curious Bishop youngster by the name of Harry Matlick was shown the gravesite by his pal Harry Shaw. Matlick told his school chums it was "only an indention in a pasture."

Bill Chalfant, the inveterate chronicler of the people and events of the Owens Valley, vividly described the Monte Diablo incident in a chapter of his popular *The Story of Inyo* written in 1922, fifty-one years after the convicts were made to atone for their crimes.[8] His father, P. A. Chalfant, the founder and publisher of the newspaper, may have written the "face to the moonlight" description quoted above.

---

[8] Chalfant, *The Story of Inyo*, p. 251, et. seq.

William A. "Bill" Chalfant (1868 - 1943), editor and publisher of the Inyo Register. Judging by the calendar (the year is unclear), the photograph was probably taken in 1942. (Courtesy of Laws Museum)

Working in the print room of the Inyo Register, c. 1925. The flash-back is in the original photograph. (Courtesy of Laws Museum)

This picture of a pack train at Bishop Creek, c. 1880, provides a glimpse of the look and dress of men in the community around the time the incidents described in this book occurred. (Courtesy of Laws Museum)

EPILOGUE

1
Renaming the Landscape

The fatal affair in Monte Diablo Canyon is part of the lore of the Eastern Sierra. Over the years, Mono and Inyo County locals, and eventually visitors, came to speak of the incident in such descriptive phrases as "the gun battle at the lake where the convicts were trapped." Eventually it became "the convicts' lake," and, in time, simply "Convict Lake."[1]

In much the same manner, Monte Diablo, the rugged peak towering over the lake, came to be referred to as Mount Morrison in honor of the merchant from Benton killed in the battle. United States Geological Survey maps of the area soon showed "Convict Lake" and "Mt. Morrison." By 1914 the USGS area map had become the Mt. Morrison quadrangle. Monte Diablo Canyon, as used in the title of this book, is now shown as Convict Canyon.

In later years, as the story was told and retold, there was the growing feeling that Mono Jim, the Indian guide killed along with Morrison, had been slighted. Thus, the lower peak to the north and in front of Mt. Morrison (when viewed from the outlet of Convict Lake) came to be referred to by locals, and appropriately so, as "Mono Jim Peak." It has had that designation in the USGS Geographical Names Information System since at least 1987, although the name had been used by locals for years by then. The current Convict Lake quadrangle identifies both Mt. Morrison and Mono Jim Peak by name.

The date of the gun battle has been a matter of some confusion. A plaque describing the battle placed at the outlet of Convict Lake by E Clampus Vitus and the Mono County Board of Supervisors states that the date was September 17, 1871. That is not correct; that was the day the convicts escaped from the prison in Carson City, some 150 miles north.

Sierra chronicler Francis P. Farquhar in *Place Names of the High Sierra* under the heading "Convict Lake" correctly says the battle

---

[1] The lake's original Indian name, Wit-So-Nah-Pah, is now the name of a beautiful lake six or so miles up Convict Canyon near the base of Red Slate Mountain. It's a most attractive camping spot for backpackers.

took place on September 24, 1871 (Sunday), but under the heading "Mount Morrison," he says the date was September 23, 1871. In both cases he cites the first edition (1922) of Bill Chalfant's *The Story of Inyo* as his source.

The date of the gun battle was, in fact, Sunday, September 24, 1871. This can be determined by a careful reading of the newspaper articles describing the pursuit of the convicts. Esmeralda County deputy sheriff Palmer of Aurora wrote his note to Mono County deputy sheriff Hightower on the afternoon of Friday, September 22, while at the way station at Adobe Valley. He sent a rider fifteen miles to Benton to deliver the note, whereupon deputy Hightower set about forming a posse. The Esmeralda and Mono groups then met the next day, Saturday, at Hightower's mill in the Glass Mountains. Morrison saw the convicts start up Monte Diablo Canyon late that day, and the Mono posse spent the night at the McGee ranch. The gun battle was the next day, Sunday, September 24, 1871.

This is further confirmed by an article in the September 30, 1871, issue of the *Inyo Independent*. It states that on receipt of Palmer's note that Friday, "Harry Devine and Mr. McLaughlin started almost immediately for Adobe Meadows, leaving Mr. Morrison and George Hightower to come on [to Adobe Meadows] with their party in the morning [Saturday, September 23], the first two taking all the available fire arms in the place [Benton Hot Springs]."

The confusion over the date has been caused by what appears to be a typographical error in the first edition of Chalfant's *Story of Inyo*; the error is carried through in subsequent editions. Chalfant states that Morrison "first sighted the men in the evening of Friday the 23rd" (Chalfant, pp. 252–3). However, the twenty-third of September in 1871 was a *Saturday*. He had the date of the first sighting of the convicts correct, but the day of the week wrong. He then goes on to say the gun battle was the next day. The next day, of course, was Sunday the twenty-fourth. Farquhar carried the error through at one reference point by stating the date was the twenty-third, but he got it right at the other. Wikipedia repeats the wrong date by citing Farquhar's incorrect reference.

Peter Browning in *Place Names of the Sierra Nevada* agrees that the date of the battle was Sunday, September 24, as do Hoover and

Kyle in their *Historic Spots in California*. Williams, without references, uses the erroneous September 23 date.

It should be clear. The gun battle at Monte Diablo (Convict) Canyon took place on *Sunday, September 24, 1871*.

2
Two Vile Men

On his return to the custody of the guard, eighteen-year-old J. B. Roberts was taken to Camp Independence for treatment of his wounds. He was closely guarded to prevent his being taken by citizens, whose thirst for vengeance had not been mollified by the lynching of Morton and Black.

The October 15, 1871, issue of Carson City's *Daily State Register* reported that his "thigh wound is somewhat dangerous owing to the fact that gangrene set in before medical aid could be obtained, but the surgeon thinks he can save the leg and have Roberts in traveling condition within a month." The surgeon did his job well, because just over a week later, Hubbard and Nesmith, the two Carson City men who had been on the trail of the convicts for five weeks, took possession of Roberts at Camp Independence to transport him to Carson City and collect the reward. It was a ride of close to 200 miles. The newspaper reported that they had their man back in prison by October 27.

Getting Roberts to Carson City wasn't without its risks. As the party approached Aurora on the second day of travel, Hubbard rode ahead to make sure the coast was clear. Learning from a jailer that the citizens would hang the young man if they could take him, the decision was to take a circuitous route and keep moving. In another move to evade detection, the party left the Esmeralda Road just prior to reaching the Wellington station, circled the station, and took the back way north through the Pine Nut Mountains to Carson City, the reverse of the route the convicts had taken as they fled south a month earlier.

The *Daily State Register* said it wasn't surprising that Hubbard and Nesmith hadn't given Roberts up to vigilantes. They're "not men to be wheedled into a surrender [of a prisoner] and both are strangers to fear."

On his being turned over to Deputy Marshal Slingerland, Roberts was described by the newspaper as being "as cheerful a young scoundrel as we ever saw in limbo." He told his captors that "it is not much of a job to get out of our State Prison, but ... after getting out the trouble commences."

His youthful demeanor had saved Roberts. But he was anything but a pawn in the hands of the older convicts, as his Bishop captors had thought him to be. In telling the story of Roberts's confession after he was captured in the canyon above the Birchim place, the *Register*'s issue of October 13 gave a startlingly different picture of the young man. (By happenstance this was the same day that F. M. Isaacs died. He was the guard who had lingered so long after having had his leg amputated as a result of wounds suffered during the battle at the prison.)

> Roberts' story doubtless sounded very well—coming from a boy—to his stern but big-hearted captors; but had they known, as those that have known him for years do, that he is one of the most heartless and hardened villains who ever wore a chain, it would have sounded differently. His captors did not know that on the night he robbed the Susanville stage he also robbed the (as he supposed) mortally wounded body of the boy whom he had persuaded to help him, and abandoned him in the sage brush to die of his wounds or be captured himself taking the whole of the money stolen and the other boy's horse. Lea. Morton was an angel, compared with Roberts—but little older in years and but as an infant beside him in iniquity.

Roberts was returned to the state prison by order of the federal district court. His original conviction for stage robbery was appealed to the Nevada Supreme Court and overturned on technical grounds. After serving two years for escape, he was released in 1873, still just twenty years old.

The Fatal Affair in Monte Diablo Canyon

Nothing definitive is known about Charlie Jones after he took off just before the gunfight in Monte Diablo Canyon. One rumor was that after receiving help from his friends in Bishop Creek, he set out for Death Valley, 150 miles to the southeast. Calling Jones the "fiend incarnate," the *Inyo Independent* quelled the rumor: "There is no truth to this we are sorry to say. He was not chased into Death Valley, and we are sorry to think he has not yet reached the valley of Death."

Another rumor was that Jones met up with Burke and Cockerill on the way to Silver Peak and they killed him, leaving his body in a cabin in Fish Lake Valley. That was also shown to be untrue.

Yet another bizarre story had him crossing the Sierras at Mammoth Pass and reaching a sheep ranch near Visalia on the western slope of the mountains. The story goes that he was trailed there by one of the men who had captured Morton and Black. Jones purportedly heard the man telling people at the ranch that Jones was an escaped convict who was going to be transported back to prison.

Hearing this, Jones, so it was said, grabbed a Henry rifle—the other man had one as well—and they engaged in a prolonged shootout that killed both of them, each being shot multiple times at close range. It was said to have been witnessed by the man who owned the sheep ranch.

That would have caused a sensation and could easily have been verified, but nothing came of what was nothing more than a fanciful rumor. The mystery is how such a story got started in the first place, given that close-range shots from a Henry striking a man nearly anywhere in the body would disable if not kill him. Moreover, the men who trailed the convicts were from Carson City, and that city's newspapers, which reported the prison escape and subsequent murders in detail for months, never ran a story saying that one of its residents was killed in a shoot-out with Jones.

Jones remains a missing man in the annals of the Nevada State Prison. With the exceptions of dead men Morton and Black, he was the only one of the twenty-nine escapees who wasn't returned to prison. Yet he was the most blameworthy of the crew. If ever a man deserved a visit from the citizens' safety committee, it was Charlie Jones. Justice would have been best served, however, had he suffered the ignominy of a trial in front of a jury of citizens, knowing all the while that a hangman's knot would soon break his neck.

3
Vigilantism

The Oxford English Dictionary defines "vigilante" as a "member of a self-appointed group of people who try to prevent crime or disorder in a community where law enforcement is imperfect or has broken down." That has a nice, English-like, civil ring to it, but it hardly describes vigilantism in the Old West.

The law then was neither imperfect nor broken. People arrested were taken before the bar, tried, and punished if convicted. For example, the capture, trial, and sentencing of the Verdi train robbers all occurred within seven weeks after the crime, and some of the best lawyers in the western United States handled the prosecution and defense. Justice was neither imperfect nor had it broken down, and it had certainly not been delayed.

The law, however, was the last thing on the minds of vigilantes. Their goal was always simple vengeance for perceived wrongs, the law notwithstanding. Social norms were disregarded in the heat of the moment; the law was subsumed in a temporary group-think verging on hysteria. That they often held mock trials before executing their prisoners indicates they knew their actions violated the law.

Vigilantism is the theme of Walter Van Tilburg Clark's great western novel, *The Ox-Bow Incident*, and he captures the mood perfectly.[2] Cattlemen in his fictional Nevada valley were furious about a scourge of rustling that had decimated their herds. At a boisterous meeting, one of them yelled out in exasperation, "Waiting for Tyler's kind of justice, we'd all be beggars in a year!"

> "What led rustlers into this valley in the first place?" he bellowed. "This is no kind of a place for rustlers. I'll tell what did it. Judge Tyler's kind of justice ... They don't wait for that kind of justice in Texas any more ... They know they can pick a rustler as quick as any fee-gorging lawyer that ever took his time in a court. They go and get the man, and they string him up. They don't wait for that

---
[2] See Clark, pp. 34–35.

kind of justice in San Francisco any more ... They know they can pick a swindler as well as any overfed judge that ever lined his pockets with bribes. The Vigilance Committee does something—and it doesn't take them six months to get started, the way it does justice in some places.

"By the Lord God, men, I ask you," he exhorted, "are we going to slink on our own range like a pack of sniveling boys, and wait till we can't buy the boots for our own feet, before we do anything?"

In the case of the Daly Gang in Aurora, a "trial" was held by the safety committee. Then, with nooses around their necks and just before the trapdoor was sprung, the accused were allowed to make statements to a hostile crowd. That was the extent of their opportunity to defend themselves. That was the extent of "justice." Ironically, two of the men would likely have been freed by a jury or found guilty of non-capital offenses.

Similarly in the case of Leander Morton and Moses Black, the vigilantes organized themselves into a self-described "jury," appointed a secretary to record the proceedings, and questioned the accused before pronouncing and immediately carrying out death sentences. The newspaper endorsed the illegal proceeding by self-consciously questioning whether the law would "ever" have meted out adequate punishment. It praised the "coolness and decision which has characterized all these proceedings." Yet as the newspaper had itself acknowledged, there were differing versions of who killed Billy Poor, Robert Morrison, and Mono Jim.

The Convict Lake affair and its aftermath thus presaged and was nothing short of a real-life *Ox-bow Incident*.

The person appointed secretary to record the proceedings prior to the lynching of Morton and Black might well have written the newspaper articles that serve as a basis of this narrative and provided its title. The detail in the stories seems too precise to be based on hearsay, and the writing style is one of immediacy, of being intimately familiar with the facts; indeed, of being there in person.

In addition to the fact that many innocent people were lynched or that, like it or not, it was part of the culture of the outback west, the ultimate problem with vigilantism was that it nearly always left critical unanswered questions. As shown here, it may well have been that certain well-known citizens of Bishop Creek had aided and abetted the convicts and were therefore complicit in the murders of at least three men. The actions of the vigilantes assured that the truth would never be known.

Bibliography / Recommended Reading
Books and Articles

Ambrose, Stephen E. *Undaunted Courage*. 1st Touchstone ed. Simon and Schuster, 1977.

Ambrose, Stephen E. *Nothing Like It in the World*. 1st Touchstone ed. Simon and Schuster, 2001.

Bain, David H. *Empire Express: Building the First Transcontinental Railroad*. New York: Penguin Books, 1999.

Bell, William, *The Reno Gang's Reign of Terror*. Wild West Magazine, August 29, 2007.

Brown, Richard M. *Strain of Violence: Historical Studies of American Violence and Vigilantism*. Oxford University Press, 1975.

Bryson, Bill. *A Walk in the Woods*. Broadway Books, 1998.

Bryson, Bill. *At Home*. 1st Anchor Books ed. 2011.

Catskill Archive. *Railroad Construction in Old and Modern Times* (from *Scientific* American, December 9, 1893). www.catskillarchive.com.

Chalfant, W. A. *Gold, Guns & Ghost Towns*. Chalfant Press, Inc., 1975.

Chalfant, W. A. *The Story of Inyo*. rev. ed. Bishop, CA: Community Printing and Publishing, 1975.

Clark, Walter Van Tilburg. *The Ox-Bow Incident*. Random House, 1960.

Davis, Sam P. *The History of Nevada*. Elms Publishing, 1913.

Donald, David Herbert. *Lincoln*. 1st Touchstone ed. Simon and Schuster, 1995.

Egan, Ferol. *Fremont: Explorer for a Restless Nation*. University of Nevada Press, 1985.

Elliott, Russell R. *History of Nevada*. 2nd rev. ed. University of Nebraska Press, 1987.

Farquhar, Francis P. *History of the Sierra Nevada*. University of California Press, 1972.

Farquhar, Francis P. *Place Names of the High Sierra*. Sierra Club Publishing, 1926.

Farquhar, Francis P. *Up and Down California in 1860–64*. University of California Press, 1966.

Galloway, John Debo. *The First Transcontinental Railroad: Central Pacific, Union Pacific.*, Simmon-Boardman, 1950.

Hillgartner, Del., Family History: Reno, *John Reno, The World's First Train Robbery*, (2000-internet available).

Hulse, James W. *The Silver State*. 2nd ed. University of Nevada Press, 1998.

Kinkead, James H. "The First Train Robbery on the Pacific Coast." *Third Biennial Report of the Nevada State Historical Society*. Carson City, NV: State Printing Office, 1913.

Lillard, Richard G. *Desert Challenge: An Interpretation of Nevada*. 1st ed. Alfred P. Knopf, 1942.

Mack, Effie. *Mark Twain in Nevada*. Chas. Scribner & Sons, 1947.

McCrum, Robert, Robert MacNeil, and William Cran. *The Story of English*. 3rd rev. ed. Penguin Books, 2002.

McGrath, Roger D. *Gunfighters, Highwaymen & Vigilantes*. University of California Press, 1987.

McLure's Magazine."The Destruction of the Reno Gang," Vol. 4, December 1894–May 1895, from the library of the University of Michigan Press.

McPhee, John. *Basin and Range*. New York: Noonday Press, 1981.

Morris, Roy, Jr. *Lighting Out for the Territory: How Samuel Clemens Headed West and Became Mark Twain*. Simon and Schuster, 2010.

Nation, Nyle. *The Pine Nut Chronicle*. 2nd ed. Pine Nut Press, 2000.

Nevins, Allan. *Fremont: Pathmarker of the West*. University of Nebraska Press, 1992.

Sifakis, Carl. *The Encyclopedia of American Crime*. New York: Facts on File, 1982.

Starr, Kevin. *California: A History*. Modern Library Compact Edition, 2007.

Stewart, Robert E. *Aurora: Nevada's Ghost City of the Dawn*. Nevada Publications, 2004.

Thompson and West. *History of Nevada, 1881, With Illustrations*. Edited by Myron Angel. Berkeley, CA: Howell-North, 1958.

Twain, Mark. *Roughing It*. University of California Press, 1993.

Williams, George III. *The Murders at Convict Lake*. Tree by the River Publishing Trust, 2000.

Wilson, R. Michael. *Great Train Robberies of the Old West*. TwoDot ed. Morris Book Publishing, 2007.

Newspapers

Aurora Daily Times
Daily State Register (Carson City)
Esmeralda Star (Aurora)
Esmeralda Daily Union (Aurora)
Inyo Independent (Bishop)
Nevada State Journal (Reno)
Reno Daily Crescent
Sacramento Union
Territorial Enterprise (Virginia City)

Credits

The photograph on the cover and the photographs of Mount Morrison (Monte Diablo) and Convict Lake that accompany the text were taken by nature photographer Rollie Rodriguez of Mammoth Lakes. Originally in color, they are reproduced here in black and white for a desired effect. The cover shot is a portion of a larger photograph of the range including Mount Morrison and, to its right, Convict Canyon. Taken from Hot Creek, it shows the area traversed by the convicts as they approached the canyon. Mr. Rodriguez produces magnificent color scenes for calendars, and his work has been featured on the covers of well known travel guides.

The cover design is by graphic artist Alex Leutzinger of Reno, who has produced covers and interior designs for various other publications. After listening to the gist of the story told in the book, he came up with the ideas for the old west style printing and hangman's noose on the cover, and the black and white picture format. He was raised in the same area of eastern Nevada as the author.

The photographs of the horses of Adobe Valley and the remains of the nineteenth century Adobe Valley way station are by Nigel and Gail Smith of Crowley Lake, California. They have taken hundreds of superb pictures of the horses, to the extent that is was nearly impossible to make selections for this book. They have striking photographs, worthy of any art show, of horses rearing and fighting against a backdrop of the yellows, oranges, reds and blacks of a fading sunset.

Dennis and Lauren Funaiole, a retired NASA engineer and a city planner, are building their refuge from urbanity at the location on Adobe Creek where the evidence suggests the convicts crossed and stopped to rest on September 20, 1871. At that point the convicts were still on the historic Aurora and Owens River Wagon Road. The author is indebted to the Funaioles for their guided tours of the valley, including the areas where the wild horses congregate, and the Glass Mountains and environs. Such experiences generate wonderment at the lonely beauty of the landscape, and an appreciation of those who lived far out there when hand saws, square nails, and horse-drawn wagons were the primary labor-saving devices and a fast horse the best means of communication.

The Author

Jim Reed was raised in a company mining town in the mountains of eastern Nevada's White Pine County near Great Basin National Park. He presently lives in the lofty reaches of California's Eastern Sierra near Yosemite National Park. He graduated from the University of California's Hastings College of Law before serving as chief counsel of the California Legislature's Assembly Judiciary Committee, where he helped write the state's iconic environmental quality act. He taught environmental and constitutional law, served on various special legislative committees and in local government, and spent a decade on the governing board of the bi-state Tahoe Regional Planning Agency. He is a partner in the firm of Liebersbach, Mohun, Carney & Reed in Mammoth Lakes, specializing in public and environmental law.

He has spent much of his life backpacking and peak climbing. His paradise is the environs of Silver King Creek, nestled among the peaks south of Lake Tahoe.

This book is dedicated to his sons, who are backpackers and marathon runners. It was written in memory of his parents, who came from pioneer Nevada families, and for his sister.